THE BOSTON

CELTICS

THE BOSTON

THE HISTORY
LEGENDS, AND
IMAGES OF
AMERICA'S MOST
CELEBRATED
TEAM

BOB RYAN

PHOTOGRAPHS
BY
DICK RAPHAEL

CELTICS

▲▼ Addison-Wesley
Publishing
Company, Inc.

Reading, Massachusetts
Menlo Park, California
New York
Don Mills, Ontario
Wokingham, England
Amsterdam
Bonn
Sydney
Singapore
Tokyo
Madrid
San Juan

Library of Congress Cataloging-in-Publication Data

Ryan, Bob, 1946–
    The Boston Celtics: the history, legends, and images of America's
most celebrated team / Bob Ryan and Dick Raphael.
        p.   cm.
    ISBN 0-201-15326-2
    1. Boston Celtics (Basketball team)—History. I. Raphael, Dick.
II. Title.
GV885.52.B67R9   1989
796.323'64'0974461–dc20   89-36058

The text editor was Mark Starr.
The Boston Celtics was designed by Bob Ciano.
The design assistance was provided by Robin Michals.
Production was coordinated by Pond Press.
Type was set in 9.5/12 Bookman Light, condensed 10 percent, by Cosmos of
Long Island City, New York.
The color separations and camera work were supplied by Lehigh Press
Colortronics of Elk Grove Village, Illinois.
Von Hoffmann Press of Jefferson City, Missouri, printed and bound the
book on 65-pound Warrenflo stock from Lindenmeyr Paper Company.

The photographs in this book—and more—are available from
Dick Raphael Associates, Sports Photography,
132 Beverly Street, Boston, MA 02114.

Jacket design by Copenhaver Cumpston.
Jacket photographs by Dick Raphael.

ABCDEFGHIJ-VH-89
First printing, September 1989

● To Red Auerbach and the players and coaches of the past 25 years, for all the thrills you've given me and the great scenes you've presented to my cameras. To the late Howie McHugh, legendary P.R. Director, who allowed a kid to take photographs in the Garden. To K.C. Jones and Jan Volk, friends for more than 20 years. To Mark Starr. To Jeff Cohen. To Jeff Twiss, David Zuccaro, and Wayne Levy, the Celtics' superb Public Relations staff. To Tod Rosensweig, Vice-President of Marketing; Steve Riley, Vice-President of Sales; and Joe DiLorenzo, Vice-President of Finance. To Duane Johnson and Joe Durkin. To Mary Faherty, Millie Duggan, and all others in the Celtics office who have been so helpful and kind over the years. And finally, to my mother and father.

Dick Raphael, May 1989

● You're 23 years old and six months removed from second balcony spectator status. You need help in learning what the NBA is all about. If you're lucky, as I was, you get it from Tom Heinsohn, Red Auerbach, John Havlicek, Don Nelson, Satch Sanders, John Killilea, and Paul Silas. You get it from Jeff Cohen, Jan Volk, and the late Howie McHugh. You get it from NBA sources such as Dave DeBusschere, Billy Cunningham, Pat Williams, and any number of NBA players, coaches, general managers, and scouts. And you get it from *Boston Globe* editors such as the late Jerry Nason, Ernie Roberts, and Dave Smith, who gave the kid a chance.

Bob Ryan, May 1989

CONTENTS

DOUBT THAT EVEN IN HIS WILDEST DREAMS, WALTER BROWN COULD HAVE IMAGINED that the team he founded in 1946 would become one of the most dominant and storied teams in sports history. The Celtics have now enjoyed 43 years in Boston, and I've been here for 39 of them. During that time, we've won 16 championships, and we and the fans of Boston have been privileged to watch the finest basketball ever played in the NBA.

The Celtics have been, more than anything else and from the top down, a family. Although we have had various types of ownerships over the years, the one constant they have shared is a concern for the welfare of the team and for the way it performs on the court. Current owners Don Gaston and Alan Cohen and Paul Dupee are a perfect case in point. Not only are they above-average basketball fans themselves, but they also fully understand and appreciate the complex problems facing teams today, problems that are very different from those of past eras. And nothing better illustrates the family nature of the Celtics than current General Manager Jan Volk's career with the team. Jan has spent his whole adult life involved with the Celtics, gradually moving up to take full control of its operations. The great support of owners and continuity among management have created the sort of stable environment that has allowed the Celtics to flourish.

It's no surprise that such athletic and managerial excellence would have attracted journalistic talent to match. Thousands of photographers and reporters from newspapers and magazines all over the country—and around the world—have recorded the team's exploits, and I've gotten to know many of them. In the past 25 years, however, I have to say that two stand out: Dick Raphael, the team's official photographer, and Bob Ryan of *The Boston Globe*. Before their professional careers began they were fans, while the Celtics' dynasty of the '50s and '60s was being built. Nobody could produce a better history of this team than Bob Ryan and Dick Raphael.

It seems as though Dick Raphael has been here forever. In fact, he first started bringing his camera to Celtics games at the Garden in the early 1960s, when he was still a student at Boston University. Of course, I didn't know him personally then as my responsibilities were on the court, not in the front office. He would make his way down to the floor, usually under one of the baskets, and photograph the action—and after a while I came to recognize him. I remember he always had the latest equipment and obviously took his work seriously. I didn't know that what he really wanted was to be the team's photographer.

The problem for Dick was that Walter Brown didn't like photographers. Walter attended a lot of games, and whenever he'd spy Dick, he'd send someone down to escort him from the Garden. Dick was persistent, but Walter owned the team. During his visits to the Garden, Dick got to know Howie McHugh, the legendary Celtics public relations chief of that era. Howie liked Dick and recognized his talent. We were then in the midst of our amazing streak of 8 NBA championships in a row, and Howie also recognized the Celtics' crying need for an official, day-in day-out team photographer to record its remarkable history. Howie convinced Walter to hire the young man he'd been throwing out of the Garden, and Dick has been part of the organization ever since.

Bob Ryan had an easier time connecting with the Celtics, though he, too, won the job because of his obvious talent. He had spent one summer at the *Globe* as an intern, and when he applied for a full-time job in the summer of 1969, he was handed the Celtics beat. I can tell you that few Celtics rookies have had such a fast start.

In many ways, Bob couldn't have picked a worse time to start covering the Celtics. Bill Russell and Sam Jones had just retired after the team had won one of its most difficult championships. The '69–'70 team only won 34 games, losing 48. For a city and a media corps—much less for a team—that had enjoyed 11 championships in the previous 13 years, this must have been hard medicine. However, the turn-around was quick: Dave Cowens arrived at the start of the next season, and Bob soon found himself reporting on a new Celtics era. In my view, there have been three distinct eras (Larry Bird's being the third), and Bob has been there for two of them.

Dick and Bob are true students of the game of basketball. Sure, they've had the advantage of watching night after night. But they've also made it their business to know personally, and to study, our players, the opposition, the referees, the coaches. In this way, Dick can anticipate a certain player's moves and is in the right position to snap one of his classic photographs; and Bob knows what to expect from a particular player and from the team during a given game, and therefore how to report on their performances. Try taking an action photograph sometime, or writing your own column about the previous game—under deadline—and you'll see how talented and experienced these two really are.

I must say I'm a great fan of Dick's photographs—so much so that I have a number of them framed at home and in my office. And I'm not alone. You'll find Dick's photographs framed in bars and offices all over Boston. And *Sports Illustrated* regularly "borrows" him to cover New England sports events. Not only do his images capture moments of great drama and emotion, but they are invariably perfectly composed. This speaks to Dick's impeccable timing. He has saved his best for some of the greatest individual confrontations in Celtics history, which Bob recounts in his history: the photograph of Bill Russell blocking Wilt Chamberlain's finger-roll, which is one of the greatest sports photographs of all time; the one of John Havlicek driving past Jerry West; or of Larry Bird paired off with Julius Erving. Every time I see one of Dick's photographs, it evokes strong memories for me. I'm sure the remarkable photographs in this book will do the same for you.

I can't say that I've *always* agreed with everything Bob Ryan has written about the Celtics—but I *can* say that I've always respected him for his opinions and admired the fact that he was willing to express them. And after all, one can't possibly ask more from a relationship with a reporter. As much as one should have with a reporter, I have a friendship with Bob. Like him, his children have grown up around the Celtics, and his son even attended my basketball camp.

Bob is a very fine writer, and his ability to churn out graceful prose, game after game, has put him at the top of his profession. His hallmark is his love for and understanding of basketball, so that even when he says something I don't agree with, I know he must have a good reason for saying it. You may disagree with him, too. You may think that in this book he has focused on one player more than another, that he hasn't, perhaps, done justice to one of your heroes. But know this. As with everything he writes, his history of the team comes from personal observation; and I can honestly say that no journalist writing today has more perspective on or more insight into the Celtics. He is objective and fair, and he has always honored the basic principles of teamwork and fellowship that have made this team great.

As you look through this book, try to imagine yourself behind Dick's camera or at Bob's post at courtside. They have rekindled many of my greatest memories, moments I know many of you have shared. I hope they are around to chronicle the next quarter-century of the Boston Celtics' saga.

Red Auerbach

1 BEGINNINGS

COURTESY THE BOSTON CELTICS

The first Celtics team, 1946–47. Back row (l. to r.): Trainer Harvey Cohn, Al Brightman, Art Spector, Harold Kottman, Connie Simmons, Gerard Kelly, Assistant Coach Danny Silva. Front row: Dutch Garfinkle, Charlie Hoefer, Coach John "Honey" Russell, John Simmons, Wyndol Gray.

© JERRY BUCKLEY

Bob Cousy, Bill Russell, Red Auerbach, and Walter Brown.

**M**OST PROFESSIONAL BASKETBALL teams are loved by their hometown fans. Only the Boston Celtics are beloved throughout the world. The Celtics have followings in Italy, Spain, Belgium, France, the Scandinavian countries and throughout South America. Celtics T-shirts have shown up in photographs from the jungles of Nicaragua to the mountainous regions of the Soviet Union. Other teams have histories; Boston alone has a mystique.

The city was an unlikely place to spawn a basketball legend. New York, Philadelphia, Chicago and other eastern and midwestern cities had basketball histories dating from the 1890s. But even though the game had been invented not too far away in Springfield, Massachusetts, the city of Boston emerged from World War II with virtually no awareness of the game. Its school system had dropped the sport in 1925, which meant that thousands of Bostonians had grown up with no basketball in their sporting diet.

The Celtics were born into this spectator vacuum in 1946. Their *padrone* was Walter Brown. As president of the Boston Garden, he joined with fellow arena entrepreneurs to form the Basketball Association of America, primarily to have something to put in their buildings when there wasn't a hockey game, prize fight or track meet. Fostering the game of professional basketball was strictly a secondary consideration.

Walter Brown knew little about the game beyond the fact that the ball was round. For the first four years of the team's existence — two with John "Honey" Russell as coach and two under Alvin "Doggie" Julian — the Celtics were both an artistic and a financial failure. The club made the playoffs only once and never attracted as many as 5,000 fans to a game. But despite the monetary drain, Brown grew to love his team. Perhaps it was entrepreneurial pride, or just plain stubbornness. Regardless, Brown became a truly devoted owner.

The watershed year for the Celtics was 1950, when two men arrived in Boston to shake the team and the city out of their basketball lethargy. The first was the new coach, the team's third in five years. Brown may have known nothing about the game, but he *knew* he knew nothing. He took the advice of *Boston Record* sports editor Sam Cohen and hired a brash, irascible, immodest 32-year-old whose birth certificate identified him as Arnold J. Auerbach, but whose friends and enemies — then, as now, about a 50-50 split — knew him as "Red." Auerbach had previously coached the Washington Capitols and the Tri-City Hawks, where he had clashed with Hawks owner Ben Kerner. A man of extreme self-confidence, he must have been delighted to discover that his new boss was a basketball neophyte who was not inclined to interfere.

The second key arrival that year was Bob Cousy, aka Mr. Basketball. His story is well known: how he won immense local fame as the star of exciting Holy Cross teams in the late 1940s; how Auerbach angered fans by bypassing Cousy in the draft and selecting Bowling Green center Chuck Share, a sturdy 6'-11" fellow of moderate grace; how, upon the demise of the Chicago Stags, Cousy's name went into the celebrated fedora along with those of veteran stars Max Zaslofsky and Andy Phillip; how Walter Brown, in one of his classic gentlemanly gestures, al-

lowed the other two owners to select ahead of him, thereby making Cousy a Celtic by default; how Auerbach scorned what he considered to be Cousy's excessively flashy style of play; how player and coach grew to respect one another; how Cousy's dynamic play kept the franchise afloat through some lean years; how Cousy finally hooked up with Bill Russell to earn six championship rings; and, finally, how Auerbach has spent the last quarter-century proclaiming that Cousy was a true original who will never be surpassed as a ball handler/playmaker/floor leader.

Auerbach's Celtics were the highest scoring club in the league in each of his first six years, but they never came close to a championship. The Minneapolis Lakers were the dominant team. Led by Number 99, the great center George Mikan, and quarterbacked by resourceful guard Slater "Dugie" Martin, the Lakers won championships in 1952, 1953 and 1954. Boston's annual fate was elimination by either New York or Syracuse. In key games, Boston seemed unable to get the ball into Cousy's hands often enough to execute the feared Celtics fast break.

The Cooz had a skilled backcourt partner in Bill Sharman, a versatile and dedicated athlete who became the premier middle-distance shooter of his era. "Easy" Ed Macauley provided additional scoring from the center position, but he was too slender to be a major factor on the boards. Kentucky great Frank Ramsey had joined the team in 1954, contributing as both guard and forward. "Jungle" Jim Loscutoff arrived a year later, adding some rebounding and a lot of defensive intimidation. Auerbach, by then the

The first Celtics coach, John "Honey" Russell, got the franchise off the ground during the 1946-47 season, and into the team's first playoffs in 1948.

Alvin "Doggie" Julian, the second Celtics coach, led them for the 1948—49 and 1949—50 seasons. His losing record of 47—81 would be quickly turned around by his successor, Red Auerbach.

A classic Red Auerbach tirade against "poor" officiating. While parading in front of the scorer's table, Auerbach often passed Celtics owners whose seats were at the table.

Red lights his victory cigar, so the game must have been locked up; Auerbach was never impetuous with his cigar. In sixteen seasons at the Celtics helm, Auerbach won nine NBA championships, the last eight in a row, whereupon he retired and turned the reins over to Russell in 1966.

Red Auerbach's favorite photograph of himself.

team's coach, general manager, traveling secretary, psychologist and father confessor, had assembled every piece of the puzzle but one.

He was already scheming to acquire that last piece. Acting on a tip from his old George Washington University mentor Bill Reinhart, whom Auerbach credited as the father of the modern fast break, Red had quietly scouted a young phenomenon at the University of San Francisco by the name of Bill Russell. The USF center had burst into the nation's sporting consciousness during his junior year, but a full year

earlier the astute Reinhart had assured Auerbach, "I just saw a kid who's going to be great." If Russell had only been a stock, Reinhart could have died a billionaire.

Russell's path to the Celtics was only slightly less strange than Cousy's. The team had only the third pick in the 1956 draft, behind Rochester and St. Louis. Rochester owner Lester Harrison bypassed Russell because he couldn't afford him. St. Louis was willing to deal, but the price was steep. To secure Russell, Auerbach gave St. Louis Ed Macauley and future star forward Cliff Hagen, a former Kentucky teammate of Frank Ramsey's just back from a stint in the army. With that, Russell

Remembered for his dribbling and passing skills, Bob Cousy was also an offensive force, averaging 18.5 points per game over his 13-year career.

In this quintet of photographs by Russ Adams, Bob Cousy's wizardry is on full display. He stops on a dime, seeing the play develop in his mind; draws both Fort Wayne Pistons defenders to him as Bill Sharman observes; and flicks a blind over-the-shoulder pass to Dwight "Red" Morrison, a substitute forward during the pre-Russell years of 1954—56, who obviously is expecting Cousy's sleight of hand. Morrison then blows past all five Pistons for the lay-up.

Left to right: Arnie Risen, Jim Loscutoff, and Dixon Hemric.

became a Celtic — and basketball was about to acquire a national identity.

Red Auerbach would never again have to lead the Celtics without Bill Russell, and the big center helped him fulfill his wildest coaching fantasies. A truly superior coach has more than rules, regulations and a playbook. He has a vision of how the game should be played. Only a very few ever see that vision realized (Red Holzman in 1970, Jack Ramsay in 1977, Pat Riley in 1987). With Russell as the driving force, Auerbach would see his basketball vision successfully displayed for ten exhilarating years.

Russell enabled Auerbach's teams to play the kind of aggressive defense and up-tempo offense Red loved. Red never saw basketball as a stand-around game, but as a game of movement and individual creativity. For years, he kept the smallest playbook in the league. The Celtics used only seven plays — and any intelligent rival knew them. The key, however, was that each play had numerous options. It was the Celtics' mastery of those options that

made them such a dangerous offensive team. For every defensive action, the Celtics were ready with a reaction.

To Auerbach, plays were secondary anyway. His favored offense was 48 fast-break minutes. Why worry about plays when you can put the ball in the hands of Cousy, the consummate improviser and decision-maker? Auerbach liked to see Cousy with the ball attacking a backpedaling defense. Tom Heinsohn, a fellow rookie with Russell, and Frank Ramsey would be on the wings, with Bill Sharman trailing slightly behind, looking to take an unmolested 15-footer. If all else failed, Russell, having rebounded and thrown the outlet pass that launched this fast break, would come streaking down the middle, looking for an over-the-shoulder dish from The Cooz that he could stuff to his armpits. For years and years, there was simply no team to rival the Celtics.

For an offensive pick-me-up or for defensive relief, Auerbach had at his disposal the fresh-legged Joneses. There was Sam, from unheralded North Carolina College, and there was K.C., who had played Robin to Russell's Batman in college. They backed up Sharman and Cousy respectively and were marvelous complements to their elders, not only because of their remarkable skills, but — even more important in the Auerbach scheme of things — because they possessed the proper attitude.

Sam waited four years for Sharman to retire before he assumed a starting role. K.C. waited five years for Cousy to step aside and turn the helm over to him. Auerbach saw their patience as a virtue, and it was eventually rewarded. Both Jones jerseys are retired and hang in the Boston Garden rafters along with those of Cousy and Sharman.

Of course, those were more innocent times. Players had no agents, and $20,000 was a good salary. There were only eight teams, and thus fewer than 100 jobs for professional basketball players. Pros tended to be pleased merely to be employed and were far less inclined to question the status quo than their modern counterparts. It's hard to imagine any player today whose skills rival those of the Joneses —or even come close—riding that bench for so long without complaint.

Selflessness was what Auerbach's Celtics were all about. It remains the standard by which all subsequent Celtics teams have been judged. The Auerbachian ideal was, "Ask not what your team can do for you; ask what you can do for your team."

Celtics teams were characterized by an absence of individual scoring leaders. The first Celtic to average 25 points a game was Sam Jones, and that didn't happen until the 1964-65 season, the ninth of the Russell era and Auerbach's penultimate as coach. Red's teams were wonderfully well balanced. There's much talk these days of the need for a "go-to" guy—someone to take the big shot at a critical point in the game. The Auerbach teams invariably had five go-to guys on the floor. If the shot was there, no Celtic was afraid to take it or, in fact, supposed to pass it up. Auerbach more often chastised his players for not shooting the basketball than for shooting it.

Did Sam Jones take more big shots than K.C.? Of course; the Celtics were pragmatic. Sam Jones was one of the great clutch shooters of all time. Likewise, it made more sense to have scorer Heinsohn shoot than enforcer Loscutoff when a basket was vital, and springing sharpshooter Sharman loose behind a pick was a better option than sending Russell one-on-one. But

Sam Jones' first step to the basket was as quick as any in memory. Here, he drives through three San Francisco Warriors.

if his shot turned up, each player was expected to take it. If he missed, he'd hear no criticism from either coach or players. The Celtics won together and lost together—and the record attests that they did far more of the former.

Auerbach recognized what so many others in the game failed to grasp— that there are very few complete players. The average NBA player makes it because he has certain offensive skills. Some live by rebounding effectively, and a select few survive on their defensive prowess. Only the true elite can claim to be talented (or interested) in every facet of the game. So Auerbach constructed his team by assembling complementary players. Rather than demean a player for his shortcomings, Auerbach flattered him by emphasizing his specialty. In Red's lexicon, he became a "role player."

The role player was a staple of Auerbach's teams from the very beginning. His first Boston role players were tough guys such as Bob Harris, Bob Donham and Bob Brannum, whose assignment was to protect the meal ticket, namely Cousy. The National Basketball Association was a very rough league in those days, and coaches placed a premium on matching brawn against brawn. Auerbach believed that it was essential for a team to be able to take care of itself. In fact, Red was notorious not only for condoning, but for actually promoting warfare, especially between Celtics teammates during training camp. His explanation: "It keeps players on their toes."

As the years passed, Auerbach broadened his definition and use of role players. He developed defensive specialists, rebounding specialists, playmaking specialists and even experience specialists. No coach or general

Bill Russell and
Red Auerbach
embrace after a
championship, the
affection between
them obvious.
Red's victory cigar
is lit in anticipation
of the celebration.

manager in the history of the NBA has had more success recycling veteran players than Auerbach. He was a master at extracting the last useful year or two from such veterans as Arnie Risen, Carl Braun, Clyde Lovelette, Willie Naulls and Wayne Embry. Salary caps made everything more complicated in the eighties, but the Celtics still managed to secure an aging Bill Walton, without whom the 1986 championship would never have been possible.

Auerbach's empire-building was made a lot easier by the fact that Russell was a true team player. He didn't count points, rebounds or blocked shots; the only thing that mattered was whether or not the team won. It was a lot easier for Red to instill the proper Celtics attitude when his star player embodied it. To Auerbach, the guy who set the pick was as important as the guy who took the shot; the player who blocked his man off the boards helped the team as much as the one who pulled down the rebound. Defense was always a "we" proposition — never "I," although a lot of Celtics have conceded through the years that the key defensive phrase was, "Hey, Russ!"

Veterans joining the Celtics found it easy to detect the difference. From Naulls to Embry to Paul Silas to Walton, they all rediscovered the fun in the game upon arriving in Boston.

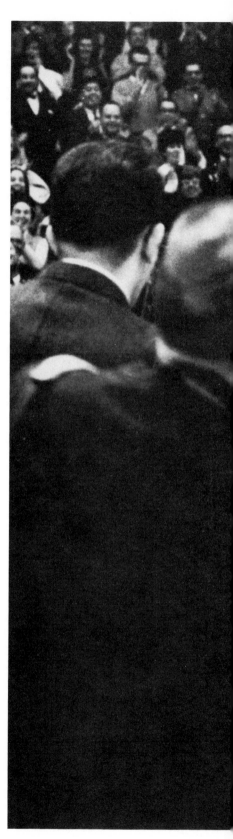

2 THE CELTICS TYRANNY

Which of Auerbach's seven basic plays is he describing?

NO ONE HAD EVER SEEN BASKET-ball as the Celtics played it in the Russell era. The Minneapolis Lakers had dominated the NBA with George Mikan as the centerpiece, but they were an old-fashioned team. Their formula consisted simply of getting the ball to Big George or bulky Vern Mikkelsen. Slater Martin was an excellent guard (Cousy called him his toughest defensive foe), but the team never ran like the Celtics.

Mikan was a true superstar, dominant enough to be acclaimed as the greatest player in the first half of the 20th century. But Russell changed the game with his defensive concepts. Players had blocked shots before, but never in such proliferation. Russell turned shot-blocking into a science — and part of his game strategy. Sometimes he swatted away lots of shots early to deliver a message. On other occasions, he allowed an unsuspecting opponent to execute his pet move unmolested for three quarters. When the unfortunate attempted that same shot with the game on the line, Russell would reject it, often triggering a Celtics fast break. Russ didn't always have to block the shot to have a deleterious effect on the opposing offense; his mere presence in the middle assured that some shots wouldn't be taken.

His teammates quickly learned how to take advantage of this uniquely gifted and cerebral athlete. Heinsohn, Ramsey and, later, John Havlicek perfected the art of sneaking away as a shot went up, secure in the knowledge that Russell would rebound the ball and throw a perfect outlet pass either directly to them, or first to Cousy. Those early Celtics teams executed more successful fast breaks in which the ball never touched the floor than any other team in history.

The Celtics won their first championship on Sunday, April 13, 1957, at the Boston Garden, defeating the St. Louis Hawks in what some afficionados contend was the most nerve-wracking Celtics game ever. It went into double overtime. With one second remaining and Boston ahead 125 to 123, St. Louis player-coach Alex Hannum fired the ball the length of the court. It hit the backboard and bounced into the hands of Hawks star Bob Pettit, who in one motion got off a final shot. The ball rolled off the rim, making the Celtics world champions on the first of 16 occasions.

The Celtics' rookie tandem was incredible. Before fouling out, Russell managed 19 points and 32 rebounds.

Vintage Russell, driving against Wilt when Chamberlain was with San Francisco.

Bob Cousy threads the needle to a cutting Sam Jones against the San Francisco Warriors.

Tom Sanders, the
conquering hero, is
carried off on the
shoulders of an
exuberant crowd
after a Celtics
championship.

"Tommy-Gun" Heinsohn scored a game-high 37 points and hauled down 23 rebounds. Their best efforts were required because the vaunted Celtics backcourt delivered its worst offensive performance of the season — Sharman was 3 of 20 from the floor, while Cousy was even worse, shooting 2 of 20. The two clutch rookies saved the day.

The Celtics failed to defend their title the next year against the same St. Louis team, primarily because Russell injured his ankle in the third minute of the third game of the series. The greatest player in the game was out of the lineup or hobbled for the rest of the series, and the Hawks prevailed in six games. Even so, St. Louis needed a sensational 50-point final game from its superstar, Pettit, to defeat the Celtics 110 to 109 in Game Six and thus prevent the series from returning to the Boston Garden.

The Celtics would win eight championships in a row before losing one again, a record unparalleled in professional sports. The string began in 1959 with a sweep of the Minneapolis Lakers. The Celtics got revenge against St. Louis in 1960 and made them pay again in 1961. They beat the Lakers, who had moved to Los Angeles, in '62 and '63, San Francisco in '64, and Los Angeles again in '65 and '66. One by one, the Celtics cast departed. Sharman said goodbye in '61. Cousy retired two years later. Ramsey and Loscutoff hung up their sneakers in '64. Heinsohn followed the next year, taking with him what Auerbach jokingly described as "the oldest 30-year-old body in the world."

By 1965, only two members of the original championship team re-

Classic Heinsohn form: about to launch his line-drive jumper over a defender's outstretched arm. Heinsohn was a scorer, averaging 18.6 points per game for his career, 19.8 in the playoffs.

K. C. Jones soars as he attempts to scoop one in against Wilt Chamberlain.

Bill Russell tries to pull his coach away from trouble after Auerbach became incensed at referee Sid Borgia's call. Public relations director Howie McHugh is in the foreground.

The Heinsohn snarl. As a coach, he became even more expressive.

the coaching fraternity one last shot at him before he retired from active coaching.

It proved to be a difficult year. Chamberlain, who had gone with the Warriors to San Francisco two seasons before, was back in Philly following a trade. The new Philadelphia team was the old Syracuse Nationals squad, rechristened the 76ers. Philly was a powerhouse team, with Chamberlain complemented by such talented players as Hal Greer, Chet Walker and Billy Cunningham. They edged out the Celtics during the regular season.

Everybody expected a tough playoff series. But the Celtics had mastered the art (or, perhaps, the science) of "second season" basketball. They brushed the 76ers aside in just five games and went on to defeat the Lakers in seven games. It was Red's eighth championship in a row and the fourth time in five years the Celtics had bested their West Coast rival. (They would do it three more times before L.A., led by Kareem Abdul-Jabbar and Magic Johnson, finally got the best of the Celtics in 1985.)

Red's final win was a 95 to 93 squeaker, the last minute played with jubilant Boston fans ringing the court. Auerbach had given his opponents one last chance to douse his victory cigar, but the stogie still glowed. Russell played all 48 minutes of Game Seven, coming up with 25 points and 32 rebounds. It was exactly the kind of performance to which Auerbach had become accustomed.

mained—Bill Russell and Red Auerbach. By then Russell had won a record five Most Valuable Player awards. His great rival, Wilt Chamberlain, won four and produced bigger scoring and rebounding numbers (blocked shots weren't an official statistic back then, so no one will ever know exactly what they accomplished in that category). But Russell is secure in his reputation as the greatest winner not only in basketball, but in the history of American team sports.

Auerbach had garnered equal acclaim. But the greatest coach the professional game had ever known was wearing out. Though just 47, he looked much older. Worse, he felt much older. The death of team owner Walter Brown in 1964 had deprived Red of his personal anchor, and he began to feel the strain of wearing so many hats within the Celtics organization. So before the 1965-66 season began, he announced that he would give

Russell's jumping ability is clearly visible here. He's on his way down with a rebound, but still way above the court.

3 RUSSELL AND FRIENDS

**Auerbach and
Russell confer in
the locker room.**

A UERBACH DIDN'T LOOK VERY FAR to select his successor. He knew the key to the team was Russell, and thus the key attribute for a new coach was his ability to get along with Russell. Auerbach left nothing to chance. He chose Russell himself.

Russell's rookie season as coach saw the Celtics championship skein stopped by the powerful Philadelphia team. Even Russell acknowledges that Philly was the best team that year. "I never thought we'd lose a playoff series — except in 1967," Russell wrote in his autobiography, *Second Wind*. With Wilt Chamberlain playing the best all-around basketball of his career, the 76ers rolled over Russell's 60-victory team in five games.

Coming off that trouncing with an aging team, the Celtics' prospects didn't look great. Russell was 32, and he was a year younger than Sam Jones. Veteran forward Bailey Howell, acquired a year earlier for Mel Counts, had turned 31. The Celtics era appeared to be over. The future belonged to defending champion Philadelphia, or perhaps to Los Angeles, which boasted the incredible one-two punch of Elgin Baylor and Jerry West.

But as so often happens, the armchair experts were wrong. Two of the Celtics' most glorious triumphs lay ahead. Russell, of course, was still the team's central figure, but on many nights the key performer was a non-starter. John Havlicek, in his sixth year with the Celtics, had inherited from Frank Ramsey undisputed claim to being the preeminent sixth man in basketball. When Havlicek arrived in 1962 from Ohio State, where he had been overshadowed by Jerry Lucas, Ramsey began tutoring the youngster in the nuances of that critical role, even counseling him to keep his warm-up jacket unbuttoned while he sat on the bench so he could whip it off and get into the game with more alacrity.

Havlicek was a superstar without a

Trainer Buddy LeRoux tends to Bill Russell before a game as K.C. Jones looks on. LeRoux was on the Celtics bench for nine seasons before moving on to bigger game as part-owner of the Red Sox and owner of Suffolk Downs racetrack.

superstar's ego. Whatever the coach asked him to do, he would try. Start? Fine. Come off the bench? That's fine, too. Guard? OK. Forward? Why not? He was, in some ways, the quintessential Celtic. Having first attracted Auerbach with his physical stamina and defensive inclinations, Havlicek gradually expanded his offensive game until he was one of the league's most productive players. He could score equally well in either a transition or a half-court game, relentlessly probing the man guarding him until he found the best way to beat him.

At 6'-5" and 205 pounds, Havlicek was an ideal swingman. He could outquick the forwards and overpower the guards. His immense physical talent had been on display at training camp with the Cleveland Browns, where the former high-school quarterback was

reputation as one of the great clutch marksmen in the game. He also had a reputation as one of the most playful men both on and off the court. He loved to tease rivals, particularly Wilt Chamberlain. When an opponent would pick Jones up on the wing or off a switch, Sam would gleefully call, "Too late!" as the shot kissed the glass and fell through.

Sam was the prototype "modern" off-guard. He stood 6'-4" in an era when most guards were closer to six feet; in his early years, he was one of the quickest players in the league. His first step was legendary. One of the prettiest sights the game has ever known was that of Sam Jones pump-faking his opponent, then gliding to the hoop and finishing off the play with a graceful one-hand scoop. Jones was also one of the last players in the league to have a two-handed set shot in his arsenal. That two-hander proved critical in the final minutes of Auerbach's last game (with typical restraint, Celtics radio announcer Johnny Most described it as coming from "forty feet away"). Sam was such an offensive threat that his defense was underestimated, but he always formed half of a harrassing backcourt duo.

At forward, coach Russell had the hard-nosed Bailey Howell, a savvy veteran and a great offensive rebounder; Tom "Satch" Sanders, the league's premier defensive forward; and Don Nelson, a classic Auerbach retread. Red had signed Nelson after the Lakers released him a few years before, and he stayed around for ten years, long enough to get his number retired to the Boston Garden rafters with other all-time Celtics greats. Nelson remains the greatest bargain pickup Auerbach ever made.

Augmenting Havlicek and Jones in the backcourt was Havlicek's old Ohio State teammate Larry Siegfried, who gave new meaning to the word "scrappy." Additional help came from former

converted to wide receiver. But his physical abilities were exceeded by his extraordinary basketball mind. If he saw his opponents run a play, he made a note of the hand signal or verbal call that initiated it. Thereafter he always got the jump on it. He couldn't understand why other players didn't retain basketball knowledge equally well. Havlicek's precise, logical mind was evident in the locker room, where he hung his socks on a hanger and arranged the bottles and canisters in his locker by height. Havlicek would trim the slightest amount of excess fat off a piece of meat with the care and precision of a brain surgeon.

The starters that Havlicek spelled included Sam Jones, whose career was still thriving despite the retirement of his backcourt mate, the other Jones, in 1967. Sam Jones, the game's leading exponent of the bank shot, had a

Two number 24s with deadly jump shots, and each named Jones: Sam and Wally.

Russell coils and
leaps against
Chamberlain in the
1968 playoffs, won
by Boston in seven
games after being
down 3–1.

University of Cincinnati star Tom Thacker, nicknamed "The Cobra," and rookie Mal Graham out of New York University, whose basketball career would be cut short by a circulation ailment.

Russell's backup, Wayne Embry, represented another Auerbach coup. The burly veteran was ready to retire after a distinguished career with the Cincinnati Royals when Auerbach sweet-talked "Wayne the Wall" into extending his career with Boston. Embry's two-year stay earned him a prized championship ring.

This Celtics team didn't run like Celtics teams of old. Its trademarks were a precision half-court offense, solid defense, tremendous cool under pressure, and an indefinable but very real sense of camaraderie and team purpose that has seldom been matched in subsequent years by any NBA team, including the Celtics.

Russell proved to be a curious boss, inattentive at practice and uninterested in details. He hadn't been much of a practice player and was even less a practice coach. No coach ever drank more coffee or read more newspapers during practice than Russell did during his three-year stint at the helm. Even during games, Celtics huddles tended to resemble town meetings, with each veteran having his say.

Fortunately, Coach Russell still had player Russell at his disposal. His major concession to age was to further limit his practice work. He still played more than 40 minutes a game (and more than 45 during the playoffs), so no one questioned his dedication. His teammates knew that the one player who could always be counted on was Bill Russell.

There was nothing complex about Russell's Celtics. They still ran Red's original seven plays, and still exploited opponents' weaknesses masterfully.

No team was better at getting the ball to the hot man or capitalizing on mismatches.

They were a bit lucky, too. In 1968, Philadelphia's great sixth man, Billy Cunningham, broke his wrist in the playoff series with New York and was unavailable for the series against the Celtics. The next year saw the Sam Jones jumper that rolled around the rim several times before falling through, tying the series with Los Angeles at two games apiece. But luck

There was nothing John Havlicek couldn't do: here he blocks Chet Walker's leaner. Hondo's jumping ability is often overlooked, but he's third on the Celtics all-time rebounding list behind Russell and Cowens.

had always been part of the puzzle. Who could forget 1962? Frank Selvy, a sharpshooter who once scored 100 points in a college game, missed an open 15-footer at the buzzer of the seventh game, and the Celtics went on to beat the Lakers in overtime to capture their fourth straight championship.

But more often than not, Celtics luck was, as baseball's Branch Rickey once put it, "the residue of design." Opponents might mumble about the leprechaun who resided in Boston Garden and specialized in redirecting their shots at critical moments. The Celtics always reasoned that any team that planned and executed as well as they did had earned a little supernatural help.

In the 1968 playoffs, the Celts again faced Philadelphia. The 76ers had captured the Eastern Division for the third year in a row and, just as they had the year before on the way to the championship, jumped out to a 3–1 series lead against Boston, with Game Five in Philly. Before that game, Russell counseled the team, "We're not supposed to win anything. Stay loose and just go out there and play the way we can." The result: Boston routed Philly 122 to 104. The Celtics were due to win one at home and took the sixth game 114 to 106. They returned to Philadelphia dead even.

Game Seven will always be remembered as the one in which Wilt Chamberlain attempted only two shots in the second half—and to this day, no one except Wilt really knows why. (Wilt's role in a seventh game would be controversial again the following year.) The Celtics ignored the screaming Spectrum crowd of 15,202, running the pick-and-roll play continuously at a hesitant Chamberlain. The final score: Boston 100, Philadelphia 96.

The final against the Lakers was anticlimactic; L.A. simply couldn't match up against Russell. The Celtics dispatched the Lakers in six games, with Havlicek scoring 40 in the final game. The Celtics were world champions for the tenth time in 12 years.

But the drama of that championship couldn't match what lay ahead the next year.

Wayne Embry earned his nickname, "The Wall," in confrontations like this one with Wilt Chamberlain. Despite a huge height disadvantage (Embry was only 6'-8"), he would keep opposing centers at bay while Russell rested. One of Red Auerbach's great pickups, Embry won a championship ring in Boston. He's now general manager of the Cleveland Cavaliers.

At the end of the 1968-69 regular season, the notion of Boston defending its title was laughable. The aged Celtics had finished a distant fourth in the Eastern Division, trailing Baltimore, Philadelphia and New York. Even if the Celtics could conceivably get out of the East, the Lakers had added Chamberlain to the Baylor-West combo, creating a three-headed monster generally regarded as invincible. In the minds of most experts, the Celtics were little more than a historical footnote.

What those experts didn't realize was that Russell had played the entire year with a "second season" philosophy. He didn't push the team, but accepted a fourth-place finish as simply a path into the playoffs. Personally, he took it easier on offense, scoring a career low 9.9 points per game, though he still worked the boards and averaged more than 19 rebounds a game.

When the playoffs began, the old geezers in green proved not quite ready for their Social Security checks. Boston dispatched Philadelphia, which had finished nine games ahead of them during the regular season, in five relatively easy meetings. New York was next, and most doubted that the Celtics — especially their 35-year-old coach — could keep pace with the young legs of such standouts as Walt Frazier, Willis Reed and Dave DeBusschere. But the Knicks proved to be a year away, and the Celtics bested them in six games as Russell dominated Reed. Only Los Angeles, Boston's opponent in the final for the sixth time that decade, stood between the Celtics and an eleventh championship.

The key game was the fourth, when the Lakers were on the verge of head-ing home with a 3–1 series lead. With time running out and Boston down by a point, Sam Jones came off a triple pick (known as the "Ohio" play because Havlicek and Siegfried learned it at Ohio State) and took a falling-down jumper that somehow found its way into the basket. The series went back to L.A. tied at two, and the teams split the next two contests.

Game Seven was a classic. Although they were playing on the road, the Celtics were loose and confident. By contrast, the Lakers were under enormous pressure. Owner Jack Kent Cooke believed a center who could match up

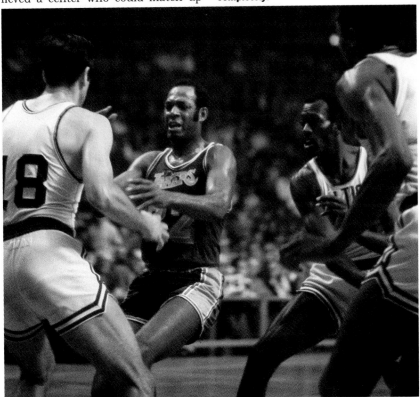

Lakers star Elgin Baylor collides with Bailey Howell as Tom Sanders moves in. As the league's top defensive forward, it was usually Sanders' job to guard the high-scoring, shifty Baylor, who was impossible to hold in check completely.

with Russell had been the one missing ingredient; the acquisition of Chamberlain was supposed to remedy that and assure a title. Cooke made elaborate plans for a victory celebration. Thousands of balloons were suspended from the "Fabulous" Forum ceiling, ready for release at the game's conclusion. The University of Southern California marching band was on hand to

Jerry West could sprint downcourt at full dribble and stop on a dime for his deadly jump shot. Johnny Most coined the phrase "he stops and pops" to describe West's speed.

Don Nelson knew where the basket was and had great touch with either hand. He was also a determined rebounder, whose positioning was more often than not perfect. A true student of the game, it's no surprise that Nellie is one of the finest coaches in professional basketball.

stoke the party atmosphere.

Early in the fourth quarter, the Celtics moved up by 17 points. Then the estimable Jerry West, who would finish with 42 points, 12 rebounds and 12 assists, led a desperate rally. Chamberlain then sustained a minor leg injury and left the game. When he informed L.A. coach Butch van Breda Kolff that he was ready to return to action, the coach, irritated that his star center had gone to the bench at such a critical moment for such a minor injury, responded, "No thanks." Instead, he stuck with Mel Counts, a one-time Celtic who was a fine outside shooter but strictly a journeyman backup center.

With a minute to go in the game and the Celtics clinging to a one-point lead, the Lakers' Keith Erickson poked the ball away from Havlicek. But Nelson picked the ball up at the foul line, and his jumper hit the back rim, bounced high in the air and fell through. The hoop proved to be the clinching basket in a 108 to 106 Celtics triumph.

The graybeards had come through. Playing in his final game, Sam Jones scored 24 points on 10-of-16 shooting. Russell, who was also playing his final game (though no one knew that for sure), was on the floor the full 48 minutes, hauling in 21 rebounds. His only regret would be that his longtime rival Chamberlain hadn't been on the floor as Russ bested him once again in the only stat that really counted.

The Celtics became the first team ever to win the NBA championship without benefit of the home-court advantage in a single playoff series. Only the 1977 Portland Trailblazers have matched that feat. The win gave Russell back-to-back championships as coach, and it would be 19 years before another team successfully defended its title. That 1969 championship may have been the sweetest of all.

Johnny Most emcees Bill Russell Day at the Garden. Legendary P.R. man Howie McHugh presents Russell with a portrait of himself.

4 LIFE WITHOUT BILL

Dave Cowens was the key to the next Celtics championship era.

A scrapping Cowens brought intensity back to the Garden.

THERE HAVE BEEN FOUR PIVOTAL players in Boston Celtics history. The first was clearly Bob Cousy. Bill Russell came next, and it's quite obvious that Larry Bird is another. The fourth was Dave Cowens, the bridge between the Russell and Bird eras and the key player in Tom Heinsohn's fascinating coaching tenure.

To say that Cowens was, and is, unique is to say that Everest is a pretty big hill. There has never been a professional basketball player quite like Dave Cowens — on or off the court. No center has matched his playing style, and his lifestyle was a strange and wonderful blend of personality, intelligence and enthusiasm for a wide variety of interests.

He was certainly a godsend to Coach Heinsohn, who had succeeded Russell in 1969 and immediately faced an insurmountable problem—the absence of Russell. He did the best job possible blending such skilled veterans as Havlicek, Nelson, Sanders, Siegfried and guard Emmette Bryant with the youthful talents of Jo Jo White, Don Chaney and Steve Kuberski.

But no amount of coaching could hide the absence of an adequate center. Heinsohn had three to choose from: Jim "Bad News" Barnes, once a Knicks first draft-pick, who was muscular but small at 6'-8"; Rich Johnson, a slender, 6'-9" kid out of Grambling; and Henry Finkel, a seven-footer who had played an honest, if limited, center for the Lakers and the San Diego Rockets the previous three seasons. Heinsohn juggled his centers as best he could, extracting 34 victories from a team that was often hopelessly overmatched physically. Boston showed occasional flashes, winning the season series from the eventual champion Knicks. But the Celts were helpless against such musclebound teams as the Atlanta Hawks.

Heinsohn made his most important first-year decision midway through

The sartorially
resplendent Tom
Heinsohn, with his
star center during
a time-out.

The sartorially
resplendent Tom
Heinsohn, with his
star center during
a time-out.

the tortuous season when he replaced his veteran guards, Siegfried and Bryant, in the starting lineup with the team's first-round picks from the last two years, Don Chaney and Jo Jo White. Heinsohn's relations with the two veterans deteriorated steadily, but in taking his stand the new coach began creating the nucleus of a future championship team.

The Boston Celtics finished out of the playoffs for the first time in 20 seasons, despite sensational years from both Havlicek and Nelson. Havlicek joined an elite group of players by leading his team in scoring, rebounding and assists (Cowens and Bird later accomplished that feat as well). Nelson popped in 15 points a game and scored a career-high 40 points one evening against Seattle.

At season's end, it was pretty obvious what the team needed. Its veteran forwards were still solid and its young guard tandem, augmented by Art "Hambone" Williams, showed promise.

The Celtics desperately needed a center. But few fans in Boston were aware of the team's eventual savior. Due to an NCAA probation, Dave Cowens' formidable Florida State team never appeared on national television during his three-year college career.

Cowens was no secret to professional scouts, who regarded him as an exceptional rebounding prospect who would probably go high in the draft. The Celtics were among his admirers, though they took pains to conceal it. Auerbach walked out of a Florida State game against the University of Dayton after only five minutes. "I made a big scene when I left so people would think I was disgusted," Auerbach confessed later. In truth, he had seen enough to convince him that Cowens was the answer to Boston's basketball prayers.

The Celtics had the fourth pick in the 1970 draft, behind Detroit, San Diego and San Francisco. Detroit's first pick was the consensus one, the great St. Bonaventure center Bob Lanier. San Diego opted for the best "pure" forward in the draft, Rudy Tomjanovich. The Warriors then surprised the experts by handing over the third spot to Atlanta in exchange for the rights to Zelmo Beaty, a former Hawks star who had jumped to the American Basketball Association. With that pick Atlanta chose Louisiana State sensation Pete Maravich. All three players picked ahead of Cowens went on to distinguished NBA careers, but Auerbach was thrilled to have another red-

head on his team. He knew the kid would be a good one. He didn't realize he'd be a great one.

Cowens quickly captured the attention of Boston fans by winning the MVP award in the prestigious Stokes game, played before each season at Kutsher's Country Club in Monticello, New York. Not far into training camp, it became apparent that the rough-and-tumble NBA game suited Cowens perfectly. The Celtics badly needed a physically intimidating player, and Cowens absolutely relished physical contact. He had the heart and soul of a middle linebacker.

The raging debate at the time was whether, at "just" 6'-8", Cowens was a center or a forward. But the kid wanted to play center, viewing it as a control-tower position, particularly on defense. Though Heinsohn wasn't ready to accede, he did say, "I don't know where this kid is gonna play, but he's gonna play somewhere."

Cowens would one day sour on his coach, but Heinsohn's daring and vision helped the young center attain NBA greatness. Dave Cowens would play center, but not in the classic mold. He followed a model constructed by Heinsohn, a model designed to capitalize on Cowens' particular gifts. It was conceived as a kind of guerrilla warfare. Sometimes Cowens would set up high; other times low. He was encouraged to run away from the bigger and slower centers and try to overpower the smaller ones. Cowens still executed some of the old Celtics plays, but also a host of new ones that took advantage of his outstanding mobility. Opponents never knew what he would throw at them.

Most of the established centers gave Cowens real trouble the first time they

matched up. After that, he battled them on equal terms on his way to sharing the Rookie of the Year award with Portland guard Geoff Petrie. Cowens' innate intelligence, combined with his tremendous strength and great drive to win, enabled him to solve the mysteries of the great NBA centers of the day—Kareem Abdul-Jabbar, Wes Unseld, Wilt Chamberlain, Walt Bellamy, Nate Thurmond, Willis Reed and his draftmate, Bob Lanier.

The Celtics were revitalized by Cowens' rebounding and fierce play from the center position. A 10-game winning streak early in his rookie season announced to the NBA that Boston's brief stint as a loser was over.

Cowens remained refreshingly unfazed by his success. Rather than sinking big bucks into a plush bachelor pad downtown, he rented a one-room cottage on an estate in the quiet suburb of Weston. He was unusually honest and always open to new ideas. In his second season, he enrolled in a course in auto repairs.

His basketball career might have been better served if he'd spent that time repairing his own game, but Cowens proved curiously stubborn about that. He never really developed his right hand, and his inside moves were definitely limited. He favored both a hook shot and a jump hook, liked to pop the medium-range jumper, and picked up scores of points on the fast break and the offensive boards. But Cowens never realized his full offensive potential.

That may be because, unlike most professional basketball players, offense was not his favorite part of the game. He much preferred rebounding and playing defense. In his strange view of the game, these were somehow more manly pursuits. Though never a dirty player, Cowens was definitely a rough one—and in his well-defined personal code of athletic ethics, that was an important distinction.

Cowens' personality and style resulted in an excessive number of fouls and fights. During his rookie season, he was called for a whopping 350 personal fouls and disqualified 15 times. Officials weren't used to such an aggressive player. He was also that rarest of species, the leaping Caucasian. Conceded Ken Hudson, a black referee, "Many of the guys can't believe a white guy can jump that high!"

Still, most of Cowens' foul problems were strictly his own doing. He was reckless and often downright illogical, which delighted the Boston fans. As majestic as Russell had been, he inspired little personal warmth. Russell has always believed that his lack of rapport with Boston fans stemmed from racism — period. No doubt racism played a role, but there was more to it. Russell had the air of a great stage actor. He would give a splendid performance and exit the arena feeling he had earned his money. He was deadly efficient, but personally cold.

By contrast, Cowens was totally accessible. It was as if the crazy kid next door had grown up and become the Celtics center. Russell had been no slacker, but Cowens was maniacal. He never conserved energy and continually tried to make every play — even the unmakable ones. The crowd loved him

Cowens was often unorthodox on offense. Here, he dribbles with the wrong hand, a spin move he often used and most often got away with because of his quickness.

for trying, and they loved the way he displayed his emotions for all to see. There were no mysteries about Dave Cowens on the court. He fought for what was his, and often for what was yours, too. He took an Old Testament approach to the game — an eye for an eye, a tooth for a tooth. He relished physical confrontations.

And he scorned deceptions. The practice of faking personal fouls, particularly faking the charge to draw an offensive-foul call, was a Cowens pet peeve. Never mind that Celtics great Frank Ramsey had made it his specialty years before, going so far as to demonstrate the practice for a pictorial sketch in *Sports Illustrated*. Never mind that Boston's current star, "Hondo" Havlicek, was one of the most notorious practitioners of this art. Cowens believed that it was immoral to fall down unless one were truly knocked down. It was honorable to take a legitimate charge, but he detested what announcer Johnny Most called "phony flops" or "Stanislavskys."

This attitude led to an ugly confrontation one night at the Boston Garden. Mike Newlin, a hard-nosed Houston guard, didn't completely share the Cowens philosophy. Early in the game Cowens got the ball in the high post, turned, and found that Newlin had jumped in back of him, flopped, and drawn the offensive foul call. Cowens was not pleased. He was even less pleased in the third quarter when Newlin successfully reprised the ploy. An enraged Cowens raced downcourt, caught up with Newlin in front of the Celtics bench and delivered a vicious forearm to Newlin's neck, knocking him to the floor. He then trotted over to official Bill Jones and shrieked, "Now THAT'S a foul!" Newlin ached for a month, but to this day Cowens defends his action as the proper response to a nefarious act.

Paul Silas rebounding against Wes Unseld of the Bullets.

by trying to outrace them down the floor or by forcing them away from the basket by drilling outside jumpers. He waged a one-man war of attrition, running relentlessly in hope that the fourth quarter, or at least the final minutes, would be his.

Cowens enjoyed great success against the game's great centers. The 1972-73 Celtics beat Chamberlain's Lakers four times in four meetings, with Cowens averaging 31 points and 19 rebounds against Wilt. During his prime, Cowens ran up a 10-game winning streak against Kareem. Lanier simply couldn't keep up with him, and seldom celebrated a victory over the Celtics while a Detroit Piston.

The first Cowens team (1970–71) won 44 games, ten more than in the previous season, but still failed to make the playoffs. Even so, the team's slide had been reversed. Cowens was the key building block at center. The gifted Jo Jo White had blossomed into a 21-points-a-game scorer, a level he maintained for the next six years until a heel injury ruined his career. Chaney, benefitting from the team's renewed emphasis on running, established himself as a punishing defensive player while scoring a solid 11 points a game. Havlicek was unrelentingly brilliant, scoring a career high 28.9 points a game. Don Nelson chimed in with 14 points a game. With this solid nucleus, the Celtics and their fans knew they had much to look forward to.

Heinsohn thought his team was ready for the 1971-72 season. He had built the club piece by piece, first reinstituting the running game with Cowens, next retooling the set offense to incorporate the talents of the newcomers and fine-tuning the defense. Another key was the return of veteran Satch Sanders, who had been limited by a knee injury to 17 games during Cowens' rookie campaign. Sanders contributed sticky defense and aggres-

The Newlin confrontation saw Cowens pitted against a smaller foe, but that was seldom the case. Down in the trenches there was a David vs. Goliath aspect to his NBA relations. Russell wasn't much taller than Cowens (an inch at most), but he certainly seemed bigger in relation to the NBA's pivot behemoths than Cowens did. Russell missed by one season the chance to square up against seven-foot, three-inch Kareem Abdul-Jabbar. Cowens fans got to watch that fascinating confrontation for ten years. Centers such as Abdul-Jabbar, Lanier or Chamberlain would try to overpower Cowens in the low post. He'd respond

sive rebounding on the floor, and wit and experience in the locker room. Boston put together a 56–26 season and won its first divisional championship since 1965. But the seasoned Knicks had too much playoff moxie, and the year ended with a disappointing five-game elimination.

Nonetheless, the Celtics were on the verge of greatness. Havlicek was the game's finest All-Around player, Cowens a unique force at center, White an All-Star guard, Chaney a superb complement to White with his defensive prowess, Nelson a steady sixth man, Williams a classic game-changer as an up-tempo guard, Finkel a useful backup center, Kuberski a nice auxiliary forward and Sanders a wily veteran.

But the Celtics still lacked a classic power forward, a rebounding and defensive force who would help Cowens do battle inside. Cowens was the only beef on the ball club. Enter Paul Silas, the product of another Red Auerbach brainstorm.

In the draft two years earlier, at the height of the NBA-ABA talent war, Auerbach had decided to use the late rounds to draft three players already signed by the ABA. One of the players whose NBA rights Auerbach thus secured was North Carolina guard Charlie Scott, who had already committed to the ABA's Virginia Squires. Late in the 1971-72 season, Scott began to make noises about jumping to the NBA's Phoenix Suns. To make that happen, the Suns had to deal with the man who controlled Scott's NBA rights, none other than Arnold J. Auerbach. The Suns had the perfect answer to Boston's power-forward problem in Paul Silas, and he was the price Red extracted for Scott. The 29-year-old Silas, an eight-year veteran, became a Boston Celtic solely because Auerbach was a step ahead of the competition — as usual.

Silas had an interesting NBA case history. The St. Louis Hawks drafted him out of Creighton University, where he was one of a handful of players ever to average 20 points and 20 rebounds over a college career (two others also played for the Celtics — Bill Russell and Kermit Washington). The Hawks were loaded with tough forwards; although Silas quickly demonstrated that he was an NBA-caliber rebounder, his playing time was limited. The Hawks dealt him to the Suns, who handed him over to the Celtics.

Just before the 1971-72 season, Silas shed 30 pounds. His disposition stayed mean, but his agility increased. Silas had decided to lose weight because he thought he was cheating himself of his athletic potential; Red Auerbach could appreciate an attitude like that.

In about the time it takes to lace up a pair of sneakers, Silas became a perfect Celtic. He proved the ideal complement not only to Cowens, but to Havlicek and Nelson as well. The old tubby Silas would never have fit into a running game. The new streamlined Silas loved to run. He would rebound the ball, pitch it out and race down the floor to take a return pass for a lay-up. He would clear out a rebound path for Cowens, who would later return the favor. He was an outstanding defender, equally comfortable guarding perimeter players or post-up men. He was also a surprisingly deft interior passer. Most of all, he possessed that most elusive of athletic qualities; he was a winner.

Silas loved to compete. To him, home games were nice, but road games were the true spice. One evening in Buffalo, at the height of the now-forgotten but then very spirited Boston–Buffalo Braves rivalry, Silas asked a reporter, "How many are out there?"

"About 18,000," he was told.

"Good," he said. "We're gonna send them all home unhappy."

More often than not, they did. The Celtics were astonishingly successful away from home during the four Silas years, winning two-thirds of their road games. The 1972-73 and 1974-75 squads each won 32 road games, an NBA record.

The Celtics have won 16 NBA championships, but ironically their best regular season ever didn't culminate in a title. The 1972-73 team started off with ten consecutive wins and never broke stride, finishing with a gaudy 68–14 record. Heinsohn's artistic vision of how basketball should be played was displayed on the parquet canvas for all to see. The Celtics ran, ran and, when the opponents were falling down from exhaustion, ran some more. "Though we didn't have a Cousy," observed Havlicek, "we ran the fast break as well as we ever did. I doubt if any of our old groups had the team speed of the '72-'73 club."

The team was phenomenally consistent. It had two 10-game winning streaks and one losing streak of two — back-to-back losses to New York on a January weekend (a playoffs omen). The team won 24 of its final 26 games, including its last eight in succession.

Cowens performed magnificently from start to finish, averaging 20 points and 16 rebounds a game while playing his unprecedented style of pivotman defense. Havlicek explained it: "Cowens established his own defensive style, as Russell had done before him. Cowens was more likely to switch

A typical Cowens offensive thrust.

John Havlicek displays the physique that led the Cleveland Browns to draft him as a receiver. He and Bill Bradley continually challenged each other as the Celtics-Knicks rivalry intensified in the late 1960s and into the 1970s.

Cowens and Doug Collins, then with the Sixers, square off.

grabbed over 1,000 rebounds, apparently without taking any away from Cowens. The duo proved the truth of the old NBA adage that when it comes to rebounding, there's safety in numbers; Cowens pulled down more rebounds (1,329) with Silas there alongside him.

The 1972-73 Celtics played with a "comin'-at-ya" swagger. They had larger-than-life personalities and an air of invincibility. But no 1973 championship banner hangs from the Boston Garden rafters. The team came up a bit short in the requisite amount of luck needed to win the NBA's postseason tournament. In the third game of the Eastern Conference Finals against the Knicks, Havlicek got caught between New York's Dave De-Busschere and Bill Bradley and wrenched his right shoulder. The Celtics lost the game and, without captain Havlicek, the fourth game as well (despite some heroics that sent the game into double overtime). Hondo returned for Game Five. Playing virtually with one arm, he scored 18 points and spurred the Celtics on to a victory secured by two clutch Silas free throws. They then won Game Six in New York, forcing a seventh game back home in the friendly confines of the Boston Garden.

The Celtics and their fans were confident. Boston had never lost a seventh game, at home or on the road. But the Knicks were a poised, veteran team and they knew what had to be done. They attacked Havlicek, whom they had treated with great deference in the two previous games, took charge early, and defeated a strangely flat Celtics team 94 to 78. New York went on to dispatch L.A. in five games for the championship.

out on forwards, or even on guards, than any center I've ever seen. Russell was in a class by himself when it came to defense, but he didn't switch out the way Cowens did. Russell would more or less discourage a person from coming toward him just by being there. He didn't have to switch the way Cowens did. Cowens got right up on the man. Russell had jumping ability, timing and an uncanny knack of knowing where the ball would come off the backboard. David's greatest trait was his ability to press a guard or a forward deep in the backcourt. Even Russell wouldn't attempt that."

Cowens' inspired play made him an easy selection as the league's MVP. But he would never have been as effective without the comforting presence of Silas. In Cowens' first two seasons, no teammate had come within 500 rebounds of his totals (1,216 and 1,203, respectively). But Silas came in and

5CHAMPS ONCE AGAIN

Havlicek and Jo Jo
White celebrate the
championship
victory over the
Bucks in 1974.

THE FIRST POST-RUSSELL CHAMPI-onship came as something of a surprise. The 1973-74 Celtics did not seem to have the drive of the previous year's model. Even though they got off to the same 30–7 start, they were only a little better than a .500 club the rest of the way and finished with 12 fewer wins than the year before.

Perhaps it was because defending champion New York, beset by injuries to Willis Reed and Dave DeBusschere, never posed a real challenge. When they met in the conference finals, the Celtics defeated the Knicks in five easy games as their great center struggled and their estimable power forward watched from the sidelines. The real challenge in the East that year came from the Buffalo Braves. Even though the Celtics won the first-round playoff series in six games, they trailed on the scoreboard for almost two-thirds of the time.

Buffalo was a finesse team built around the marksmanship, rebounding and running skill of center Bob McAdoo, the league's most prolific scorer, and the Cousy-like passing of rookie Ernie DiGregorio, a former Providence College star. Coach Jack Ramsay had instilled such confidence in the Braves that when the series began, Buffalo looked like the established team and the Celtics like the upstarts. The Braves had the talent to match their emotion. "This is one team that's even quicker than us," Heinsohn warned. "We're going to have to slow them down."

Game One set the tone for the series. For three quarters the Braves badly outplayed Boston — in the Boston Garden, no less — and led by 12 points. When the Celtics came onto the court in the fourth quarter, Cowens had entered a rather intense state his teammates dubbed "The Look." Always an emotional player, Cowens was capable

of attaining a level of intensity known to only a few athletes. With Buffalo's lead still at eight, Cowens made the play of the game. He stepped in front of McAdoo at midcourt, ripped the ball out of his hands and sprinted downcourt for a three-point play. Suddenly the momentum was all Cowens'. He scored 20 points in the fourth quarter and added nine rebounds and three blocks. The Celtics won the game by 10 points. Cowens had saved the day, and possibly the series.

The teams then alternated home-court victories until Game Six. In the final seconds with the score tied, Havlicek drove left-to-right across the key and fired. McAdoo blocked the shot right over to Jo Jo White, who picked up the ball and fired at the buzzer only to have a hustling McAdoo block his shot. But referee Darrell Garretson whistled a foul, and White, over the howls of the outraged Buffalo fans, calmly sank both free throws with no time left to win the game 106 to 104 and the series.

After that struggle, and the victory over New York, the Celtics faced one final obstacle—the Milwaukee Bucks and their brilliant young center, Kareem Abdul-Jabbar. The luck that had run against Boston the previous year was now working against Milwaukee. The Bucks were without Lucius Allen, a skilled backcourt player who had slipped on a warm-up jacket and torn up his knee. That put all the ball-handling pressure on just one guard, the great Oscar Robertson, then 34 and in the twilight of his career.

Even so, Milwaukee was favored. League MVP Abdul-Jabbar was an awesome force and Robertson, the "Big O,"

Bob McAdoo was brilliant for Buffalo in the 1974 playoffs. Five years later, he played 20 games for the Celtics during their worst season.

remained one of the most versatile and intelligent players ever to play the game. Even without Allen, the Bucks had swept a strong Chicago Bulls team in four games, prompting Bulls coach Dick Motta, a man not given to hyperbole, to label them "the greatest team of all time."

Robertson's running days were behind him, and, with the exception of wispy forward Bob Dandridge, the Bucks had little team speed. Their offense revolved around getting the ball to Kareem, who had developed amazing range with his famed "sky hook" and was canning 54 percent of his shots. His hook shot was a game-breaker and certainly the single most deadly weapon in NBA history.

Heinsohn and assistant coach John Killilea decided that the most effective strategy against the Bucks would be to try and keep the ball out of Abdul-Jabbar's hands. They hoped that a full-court press would effectively reduce the Bucks' 24-second possession to a 10-second offense. The key man was Don Chaney, because he would be guarding Robertson. If Chaney could harrass the playmaker effectively in the backcourt and make him expend valuable time and energy simply getting the ball across the midcourt stripe, the Bucks would find themselves in a hurry-up offense. Bucks coach Larry Costello had the league's largest playbook, and each set play had multiple options. But none of it would matter if Boston's aggressive defense forced the Bucks into offensive confusion.

With Chaney attacking Robertson and White applying pressure to Ron "Fritz" Williams, Allen's replacement, the Celtics set the tone in the very first quarter of the series. Boston used a series of Milwaukee turnovers to build **Though much smaller, Cowens gave Kareem as much trouble as any other center of his era.**

up a 35 to 19 lead, then coasted to a shockingly easy 98 to 83 win, a triumph all the more impressive because it took place in the Milwaukee Arena.

The series proved to be unique. There has never been another final in which the visiting team won five games (most remarkably, the final four). Nor has there been a series so

Havlicek drives at Kareem in the 1974 playoffs against Milwaukee.

completely influenced by the respective coaching duos. The 1974 Finals resembled a chess game pitting Heinsohn and Killilea against Costello and his assistant, Hubie Brown. It was check and checkmate for six games until Heinsohn & Co. came up with the definitive move. In Game Seven, the Celtics abandoned their previous strategy of having Cowens battle Abdul-Jabbar one-on-one in favor of a swarming double- and triple-teaming defense. Let one of the peripheral players emerge a hero. None could.

Before that climactic duel, there were some taut, fascinating games. Defense was the key. The highest point total by either team was Milwaukee's winning tally of 105 in Game Two—and that came with the benefit of overtime. The teams alternated victories for seven games. Milwaukee won one game in overtime and the storied sixth game in double overtime. The Bucks' resources were stretched to the limit. White dominated and so demoralized Williams that he was eliminated from Milwaukee's game plan. Jon McGlocklin, a 6'-5" outside shooter, sprained an ankle early and was ineffective thereafter. A desperate Costello transformed Mickey Davis, a 6'-7" journeyman forward, into his second guard, and Davis performed valiantly.

The truly memorable game was Game Six in the Boston Garden. The Celtics, leading the series 3–2, had rallied from six points down with just a couple of minutes left to force an overtime. Milwaukee led 90 to 88 in overtime and had possession when Chaney forced a turnover and got the ball to Havlicek. Hondo steamed upcourt and found himself one-on-one with Kareem. Havlicek wisely stopped and fired a foul-line jumper. No good. But the ball came straight back and a hustling

White, Chaney, Havlicek and Nelson line up on an inbounds play during the 1974 playoffs.

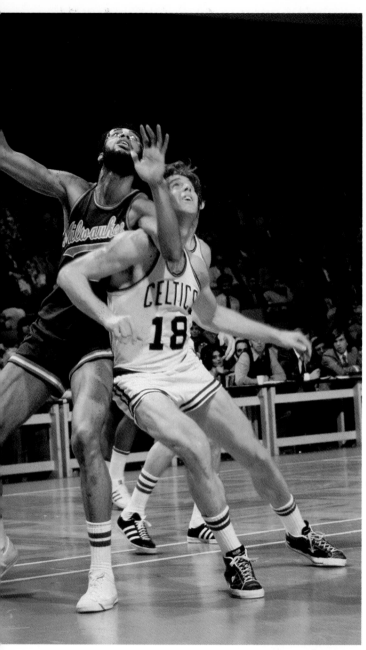

Cowens had to use muscle to contain the much taller Abdul-Jabbar.

Havlicek beat the towering Bucks center to it. He banked in a game-tying shot to force the second extra session.

An obviously charged-up Havlicek scored nine of Boston's eleven points in that second overtime, including an altitudinous baseline jumper over an outstretched Abdul-Jabbar with seven seconds to go that put Boston ahead 101 to 100. But this night belonged to Kareem. After a time out, Milwaukee got the ball to him on the right side. Cowens had forced him a good distance from the basket, and Chaney dropped off his man and almost stole the ball. Kareem ignored everything around him and began one last graceful arc, launching a 17-foot hook that swished through. The Bucks had forced a seventh game.

The Celtics brass huddled long into the night plotting seventh-game strategy. Even alum Cousy sat in. The game was anticlimactic, as Boston dominated from the start. Cowens, distressed over his 5-of-19 shooting performance in Game Six, got "The Look" early and hit 8 of 13 first-half shots. Chaney got in foul trouble early, but second-year guard Paul Westphal came off the bench to do yeoman work. Still, the Bucks managed to slice Boston's 17-point lead to three before Westphal made a sensational baseline drive. The Celtics reasserted control and won going away, 102 to 87. Cowens scored 28 points and grabbed 14 rebounds, outplaying Abdul-Jabbar, who was held scoreless for a 17-minute stretch in the middle of the game. The Celtics were world champions again — for the twelfth time and the first without Bill Russell. Asked how it felt to get to the top, Cowens replied, "I can't really say. The fun for me was in the doing." No one doubted it. Cowens had truly enjoyed battling Kareem Abdul-Jabbar, a man seven inches taller, for seven exhausting games.

The athletic Paul Westphal scored some of Boston's more spectacular baskets before being traded to Phoenix after the 1974-75 season.

That championship defined the next Celtics era. It was a tremendous achievement for Auerbach, who had rebuilt the team without the benefit of a bulging checkbook. Walter Brown was a great owner, but not an exceptionally wealthy man. The Celtics of the early 1970s were mired in financial difficulties, and Red envied the Lakers and Knicks, who seemed able to satisfy personnel needs by importing expensive players.

Auerbach's rebuilding job had begun in 1968 with the draft selection of Don Chaney, a guard from the University of Houston. Much as K.C. Jones had been years before, Chaney was overshadowed by a great big man, in this case Elvin Hayes. Red drafted Jo Jo White the following year, pulling a few strings to get the Kansas star out of the military draft and into the Marine Reserve. When he picked up Cowens, Red had acquired three starters in three years. The 1974 team started four Celtics number-one picks (Havlicek, '62, was the fourth), unusual in the NBA. Auerbach completed the job by maneuvering to land Silas, and let's not forget his Don Nelson coup. The 1974 champion Celtics represented the Auerbach genius at its zenith.

The team also represented a coaching triumph for Tom Heinsohn, who had steered an undersized team — its 6'-8", 6'-7", 6'-5" front line would be good sized for a modern backcourt — to victory over a strong team led by the dominant individual player of his age. He had the pleasure of seeing the players he had nurtured reach the peak of their profession. None was a bigger personal accomplishment for the coach than Chaney.

The 6'-5" Chaney had been drafted six years earlier in recognition of his defensive potential. But no matter how accomplished a defensive player is, he can't survive in the NBA if he's a total offensive liability. When Chaney entered the league, he was perilously close to being that. After a stint in the army, he made token appearances in 20 late-season games his rookie year and shot a dismal 32 percent from the floor. A year later, when Heinsohn paired him with White as the starting backcourt, he only managed to elevate that to 36 percent.

Heinsohn noticed that Chaney had a tendency to drift off to the side while shooting, as well as a bad release. The coach used his vast experience and considerable offensive expertise to break down Chaney's shot and reconstruct it. It was Professor Heinsohn at his very best. While he worked with Chaney in private, he kept praising him in public, assuring the skeptical press and fans that the kid with the shaky offensive game would parlay his long arms, great strength, dogged attitude and intelligence into a successful pro career. That prediction came true, and it's doubtful that Chaney could have done it on any other team in the league.

Chaney's running mate posed a different coaching challenge. The young Jo Jo White never had any problems with confidence in his offense; if anything, he was too cocky with the ball in his hands. Though sleek and agile, he had spent his college career walking the ball up in Kansas coach Ted Owens' rigid set offense. Owens' golden rule was to dump the ball inside to the big man; as a result, White's growth as a player had been stunted.

Most young players need to be slowed down; White needed speeding up. Heinsohn complained that Jo Jo preferred to move side-to-side rather than forward, and it took a while to acclimate White to the ever-forward-moving style of the Celtics. Luckily, there was never much question that White could shoot, drive to the hoop and pass. He simply had to adjust to the pro game, especially the Boston game. By the 1974 season, he had done just that.

Heinsohn called on Paul Silas to evolve into his sixth man. In the great tradition of Ramsey and Havlicek, the Celtics' sixth man was a multiposi-tional, multidimensional player who could have an immediate impact. Hav-licek appeared to be bred for the role, and no one in league history ever exe-cuted it better. Silas didn't exactly fit the classic job description. He was fun-damentally a bruising rebounder, un-likely to come in off the bench and stick a few jumpers or perpetrate a few steals. But Heinsohn recognized that there was more than one way to go about this sixth-man business. Silas could have a disproportionate emo-tional effect on the game just by the force of his rebounding presence and intimidating court style.

Of course, Heinsohn still had to sell the idea to Silas, an intelligent and proud man who knew he was good enough to start for the Celtics. More-over, he arrived in Boston with a repu-tation as a professional cynic. He wasn't into the "Celtics mystique," or any other mystique. Still, Heinsohn convinced Silas that being the sixth man was good for everyone concerned, and the tough forward came to relish his role.

The other architects of the 1974 championship felt just as good about it as the coach. Cowens, in his fourth season, was at the peak of his career. He had already collected a Rookie of the Year award, a league MVP and an All-Star Game MVP (Chicago, 1973) and was acknowledged as the finest running center in the league. Cowens was also the staunchest competitor in the pivot. When the Philadelphia 76ers selected a mythical All-NFL team con-sisting of NBA players, Cowens was the unanimous choice as middle lineback-er. Philadelphia's Fred Carter ex-plained, "Cowens is the type of guy who will block your shot and then jump on top of you." Now he had a championship ring.

Havlicek felt a different sort of satis-faction. The ring proved that there was life after Russell, something he hadn't

Cowens the rebounder. Though only 6'-8½", Cowens had springs in his legs and amassed more than 10,000 rebounds in his ten seasons, an average of 14 per game for his career. He's second on the all-time Celtics rebounding list behind Russell, who averaged a phenomenal 22.5 per game in his 13 seasons.

Don Chaney, the defensive specialist, was a key role player during the early 1970s.

previously been convinced of. Havlicek's approach to the game was so sophisticated compared to that of his new, young running mates that, even though he loved their talent and enthusiasm, he often felt frustrated. He was doubly thrilled that the Celtics not only won the championship, but won by playing with so much team intelligence.

Havlicek recalled the 1974 team this way: "We had a lot of parallels with the old Celtics, people who played their positions the way other Celtics before them had. Chaney, like K.C., the defensive specialist. Jo Jo, like Sam, the scorer. Silas, like Satch, the defensive forward and rebounder. Cowens, revolutionizing the center position in his own way as Russell had transformed it when he broke in. I was fortunate enough to be there for both teams. We had maintained the same kind of patterns to win championships in two different eras. That championship brought me peace of mind. It was really great to have the knowledge restored in my mind that we could play the game correctly."

And no one had played the game more correctly than Havlicek himself. His performance in the finals earned him the MVP award, an extension of the court wizardry he had displayed all season long. He was a coach's dream, capable of playing at an all-NBA level as forward or guard, on offense or defense. His endurance was phenomenal; at the end of his thirteenth NBA season, Havlicek was playing with as much energy as when he first entered the league.

6 END OF AN ERA

Havlicek matched up with the best of his era. Here, he shovels a backward pass away from the Sixers' Billy Cunningham.

AVLICEK, COWENS, WHITE, NELSON and Silas played together four full seasons. (Chaney departed for the St. Louis Spirits of the ABA in 1975.) With a little luck they could have won four championships; they had to settle for two, with 68- and 60-win seasons the consolation prizes in the other years.

Boston's twin calling-cards were a punishing fast break and an aggressive, intelligent defense. Almost lost to memory is how accomplished Heinsohn's teams were defensively, especially since other outfits—Dick Motta's Chicago Bulls, the rugged Detroit Pistons and the well-publicized Knicks—received plenty of attention for their defensive prowess.

When the time came to shut the opponent down, no team of that era was more adept than Heinsohn's Celtics. Other clubs allowed fewer points, but people were just beginning to understand that point total is not the best criterion for evaluating a defense. Any team can keep an opponent's score down by simply holding the ball for most of the allotted 24 seconds.

Opposing coaches recognized Boston's defensive greatness. Bob Cousy, who coached the Royals in both Cincinnati and Kansas City, rated the Celtics of that era as the best defensive team ever. "We [Cousy's Celtics teams] used to play the same way, but I'm not sure these kids don't play it better. Cowens and Chaney are just super defensively, and John digs in. I think this team is more aggressive than we were. Russell was aggressive, but not on the same terms as Cowens. Milwaukee is a good defensive team, but they don't play at the same tempo. They'll settle for picking you up at the top of the key."

Two great redheads collide: Bill Walton as a Portland Trailblazer, and Dave Cowens.

The All-Defensive Teams, selected by the coaches, reflected this appraisal. Havlicek made the first team five times. Silas made it twice. Cowens made first team once and second team twice. Chaney made second team four times (and once more later in his career as a Laker). In 1975-76, Cowens, Havlicek and Silas comprised the entire starting front line on the All-Defensive Team. That feat has never been duplicated by any team.

Despite winning 60 games, the 1974-75 Celtics were unable to defend their title, upended by Washington in six games in the conference finals. It was a huge disappointment. Cowens had missed the first 17 games with a broken foot, but his return had spurred a 50–14 finish and some absolutely brilliant basketball. With the season's end came great uncertainty. Chaney was leaving, and even though Paul Westphal was viewed as a superb replacement, Don's loss was regarded as serious. He represented so many classic Celtics virtues.

Auerbach startled the basketball world by wasting no time remedying the situation. He dealt the promising Westphal to Phoenix for Charlie Scott—the same Scott whose jump to the NBA had brought Silas to the Celtics three years before. The experts were skeptical whether Jo Jo White and the flamboyant, offensive-minded Scott could get along in the backcourt. The answer came one year later, in the form of the team's thirteenth championship.

The Celtics were not favored to win the crown in 1976. Defending champion Golden State had sustained its previous year's level of play and won 59 games, five more than the Celtics. Boston had been particularly flat in the second half of the season and entered the playoffs with no discernible momentum. But the Celtics didn't have to worry about the Warriors. They met dark horse Phoenix in the finals, mem-

Jo Jo White dances away from pressure in the 1976 finals against Phoenix, with triple overtime hero Glenn McDonald in the background.

orable for Game Five, the triple-overtime thriller often called "The Greatest Game Ever Played."

But the playoffs involved more than one game. Boston played almost identical series against first Buffalo and then Cleveland. The Celtics won two at home, lost two on the road, won the pivotal fifth game in the Garden and then took the series on the road with a strong effort in Game Six. (The win over the Cavs became easier when their center, Jim Chones, broke a toe on the eve of the series.) In each deciding game, the Celtics offensive star was Charlie Scott.

Phoenix had gone only 42–40 during the regular season, but the team had jelled during the playoffs under the skilled hand of coach John MacLeod. The Suns' key players were rookie center Alvan Adams, veteran guard Dick Van Arsdale and old friend Westphal, who had fulfilled all expectations by averaging 20 points a game. Still, Phoenix seemed a poor man's version of the Celtics, and the experts were predicting a sweep or, at best, a five-game series.

Boston easily captured the opening two games at home. The Suns won two in Phoenix before frenzied crowds, the atmosphere charged by newspaper columns suggesting that Boston's edge had been the bullying tactics of Cowens and Silas. The stories were planted by the Phoenix coach after the two Celtics stars had pretty much had their way with Phoenix in Boston. Apparently, his strategy worked.

The teams returned to Boston for Game Five. The Garden faithful weren't worried; their basic viewpoint remained, "Who are these guys anyway?" On the night of Friday, June 6, 1976, they found out. The Suns were a group of determined, gutsy players with enough poise to come back from a 22-point first-half deficit, a 15-point halftime deficit, and a 9-point deficit with just three minutes to go. They

withstood Boston's very best shot, a 38-point first quarter, and came back to tie the game in regulation at 95. It was still tied at 101 at the end of the first overtime.

The second overtime picked up in tempo. When Curtis Perry scored a long follow-up basket, the Suns led 110 to 109 with four seconds remaining. The Celtics were down to their last shot. To no one's surprise, they went to Havlicek. He got the ball in front of the visitors' bench and leaned in for a difficult, off-balance banker that went through to give Boston back the lead. Time was mistakenly allowed to run out and, after the fans were cleared off the floor, one second was put back on the clock. But the Suns had no time-outs left, so they would have to go the length of the court to score — a seemingly impossible task.

During the delay, Westphal had a brainstorm. If Coach MacLeod called an illegal time-out, the Celtics would be awarded a free throw. But at least Phoenix would then get the ball at mid-court. MacLeod did, White canned the free throw and Boston led 112 to 110. Not for long, though. Garfield Heard took the inbounds pass, whirled and launched a long-range bomb. In subsequent years, the shot has been stretched until some say it was taken from the Canadian border. However long, it was enough to send the game into a third overtime.

When this game's many twists and

Next two pages: John Havlicek has just made an off-balance jumper to give Boston the lead, 111–110, at the end of the second overtime in Game Five of the Finals against Phoenix, June 4, 1976. Paul Silas and company celebrate the apparent victory. However, one second remained, and the drama would continue as events forced a third overtime. The Celtics finally prevailed, 128–126, in the game some call the greatest ever played.

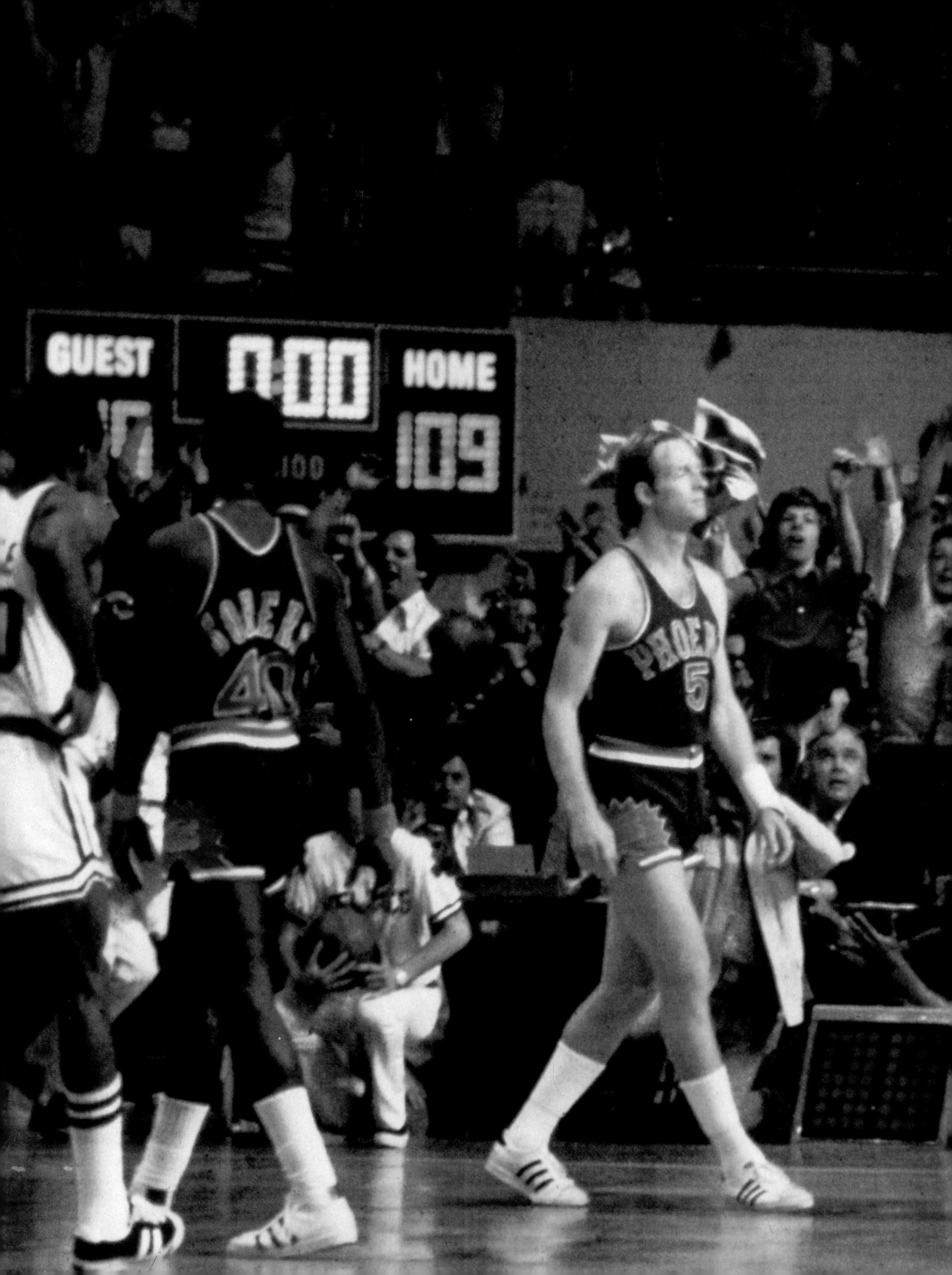
GUEST
0:00
HOME
109

turns had finally ceased, the hero was Boston substitute Glenn McDonald. The former Long Beach State star was a first draft pick in 1974, but had fallen into disfavor and was not part of the normal game plan. But after several players had fouled out, Heinsohn turned to McDonald in desperation, and he responded with six valuable points in the third overtime as Boston outlasted Phoenix 128 to 126.

Both teams were drained by the time they flew 2,000 miles and took the floor in Phoenix Sunday afternoon. But Scott, who had contributed little in Game Five, fouling out with just six points, had a little more left than most. He delivered his third consecutive clutch sixth game of that playoff season, scoring 25 points and grabbing 11 rebounds as the Celtics won the title with an 87 to 80 victory over the valiant Suns.

This was a true team championship. Havlicek struggled through the playoffs despite a torn plantar fascia in his left foot, an injury he sustained in the very first game. But the Celtics received timely contributions from every starter, and from little-name subs such as Jim Ard, Kevin Stacom and McDonald.

The triumph of '76 marked the end of an era. Before the next season, Nelson would retire and Silas would depart over a salary dispute. Owner Irv Levin would import former UCLA stars Sidney Wicks and Curtis Rowe who,

Jim Ard was a strong rebounder and occasional scorer off the bench during the mid-1970s.

**The end of an era:
two future Celtics
hall-of-famers.**

for all their big-name credentials, couldn't accept the Celtics philosophy.

The change weighed especially heavy on Cowens. Eight games into the 1976–77 season, he took an unprecedented "leave of absence" to decide what he wanted to do with his life. Without Silas by his side on the court, the game was no longer fun. It was an extreme reaction to a negative professional situation, but it was pure Cowens. He stayed away for two full months.

The team lurched into the playoffs, where it bested San Antonio in a three-game mini-series before losing to favored Philadelphia in seven games. The Last Hurrah was the sixth game, a rousing 113 to 108 win featuring outstanding performances by Cowens, Havlicek and especially White, who scored 40 points. Reality set in two days later when Philadelphia held Boston to just 77 points and won, 84 to 77. Havlicek was 37 years old. Cowens was a troubled soul. White was suffering from a bad heel. Greatness in sports is cyclical, and Boston had passed the top of the curve and was headed down; Celtics greatness suddenly seemed a long way off.

Even Charlie Scott
was shocked by
Dave Cowens'
aggressiveness on
the boards.

Charlie Scott is airborne against the Cavaliers.

7 ON THE WINGS OF A BIRD

Larry Bird and his agent, Bob Woolf, on Bird's first visit to the Garden before he signed his contract. The kid from Indiana got a warm welcome from the crowd.

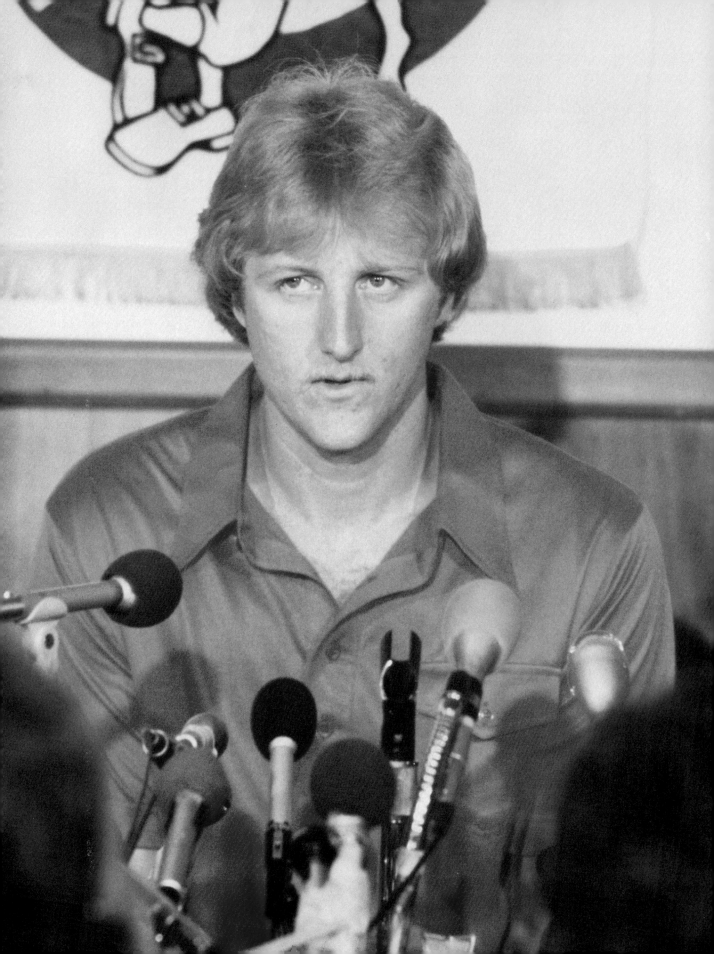

BOB COUSY SAVED PROFESSIONAL basketball in Boston. Bill Russell was the most valuable team player in the history of American sports, leading his team to 11 championships in 13 seasons (and it probably would have been 12 were he not injured during one playoff). Dave Cowens was the team's Everyman, bringing unrivaled passion to his job. John Havlicek retired in 1978 as the most complete ball player the game had yet known. But of all these Celtics, none touched the Boston fans the way Larry Bird has. The people who love the game recognize that he is the purest practitioner of the art of basketball they've ever seen.

Few in Boston expected such an impact from Bird. Despite his ample press clippings and All-American tag, his limited television exposure at Indiana State had yielded somewhat mixed reviews. He was brilliant in a late-season game against Wichita State, and he was good against Arkansas in the NCAA tourney. But some believed Sidney Moncrief had effectively shut him down and saw an omen for Bird's professional career. He was too slow, too landlocked, too white, they said. At that time, reverse racism was prevalent among many NBA clubs and fans; many thought that a white player couldn't possibly be as effective as a black player.

Whatever his limitations, Bird led his obscure Indiana State club to the Final Four in 1979. In the semifinal against De Paul he was spellbinding, sinking 16 of 19 shots. But in the championship, his first of many confrontations with the great guard Earvin "Magic" Johnson, Bird was quite mortal. He hit only 7 of 19 shots, and Magic—with a far superior supporting cast at Michigan State—ran off with the title and the MVP award.

Bird at the press conference after his contract was signed.

Two of Boston's greatest competitors, Dave Cowens and Larry Bird, only played one season together before Cowens retired.

The Celtics had drafted Bird the previous year, 1978, when he became eligible with his original college class. With an extra first-round pick courtesy of a trade with the Lakers (Kermit Washington and Don Chaney also came east in exchange for Charlie Scott), Boston owned both the sixth and eighth selections. Auerbach and company felt they could afford to gamble one of those picks on Bird's talent. Red must not have believed it was a gamble; he signed Bird for $650,000, at that time the largest sum ever handed a rookie in any sport.

If Red saw Bird as a messiah, it was because the two seasons preceding his arrival had been disasters of near biblical proportions — at least by Celtics standards. In the 1977-78 season, Boston won only 32 games. Heinsohn was fired in midseason and Tom Sanders took over the helm. Havlicek announced his retirement. He was 37 and still could play, but going to work each day had ceased to be fun. In his final game, he rang up 29 points as Ernie DiGregorio, now a Celtic and, ironically, playing his last professional game as well, kept feeding Havlicek with one spectacular pass after another.

The following year's team was even worse. Sanders lasted only 14 games before the squad was turned over to Dave Cowens, still the team's star center. The star-center-as-player/coach formula had worked a decade before, but this was a different team and era. Cowens had the Celts playing .500 ball when first-year owner John Y. Brown shocked and dismayed Auerbach by trading three first-round draft picks to the Knicks for Bob McAdoo. Red had painstakingly accumulated those picks to rebuild his squad; the team collapsed and finished at 29 and 53. Boston had hit rock bottom.

Celtics fans got through the season by convincing themselves that Red would never let the team become a perennial loser. And even before his

New coach Bill Fitch.

resigned, and Bill Fitch, who had coached the Cleveland Cavaliers for its nine seasons in the league, succeeded him. Auerbach had long admired Fitch's work and, after years of turning the team over to former Celtics players who had no pro coaching experience, was pleased to find a successful veteran coach.

In his early years with pathetic Cavalier teams, Fitch had earned a reputation as a master of the one-liner. But his wit masked a driven man obsessed with organization. He had a grasp of every coaching detail, from how to run a practice to how to set up an exhibition schedule to how much air to pump into a basketball. His Marine Corps background made him an ideal choice for a team that needed a drill sergeant.

The new coach confronted a transformed roster at the 1979 training camp. Bird's was just one new face. During the summer, Auerbach had lured free-agent forward M.L. Carr away from the Pistons. Bob McAdoo was dispatched to the Motor City as compensation. The crafty Auerbach managed to hornswoggle Detroit's coach and general manager Dick Vitale into tossing two 1980 first-round draft picks into the deal. It was a decision that hastened Vitale's successful broadcasting career. Carr proved a superb addition; he was not only a dedicated and versatile two-way player, but a tremendous boost to the mood in the locker room. M.L.'s infectious spirit lifted the team.

Cowens, grateful to be relieved of the coaching burden, decided he wanted one last big year and reported to training camp in the best shape of his career — no mean achievement for such

M.L. Carr exhibits the intensity that endeared him to Celtics fans.

arrival, Bird helped. "I was living through Bird," recalls Peter Shankman, a longtime season-ticket holder. "I remember seeing him play that game on TV against Wichita State and then sitting down on my couch and giggling, 'How did we get so lucky to deserve this?' I made Indiana State into the Celtics in my mind."

Bird was such an instant success that people tend to give him all the credit for the team's dramatic 32-game turnaround. Yes, the Celtics won 61 games in Bird's rookie season, and he deserves much or perhaps even most of the credit. But he wasn't the only fresh influence.

For one thing, the Celtics had a new coach. Cowens' assignment had always been viewed as temporary. He

Cedric Maxwell had many unique inside moves.

One of the NBA's all-time best penetrators, Nate Archibald revived his career in Boston.

a dedicated athlete. Cowens became a much more potent playing force for Fitch than he had been for himself.

Fitch also revitalized Nate "Tiny" Archibald. The aging playmaker had been a sorry sight the previous season as he tried to recover from an Achilles tendon tear; suddenly, openings he had once sped through were closed. As his on-court problems mounted, he withdrew—and Boston had deemed him a lost cause. But Fitch had too much respect for the only man in history to lead the NBA in both scoring and assists in the same season to write him off without a look. One of his first acts as coach was to anoint Archibald as his lead guard.

Fitch had two other key holdover players. Cedric Maxwell, the 1977 first draft pick, was a gifted inside scorer who had arrived full of enthusiasm. However, Max quickly discovered that he had landed not with the legendary Celtics, but with a selfish band of underachievers. Curtis Rowe, a particularly cynical veteran, told Maxwell one night after he heard him bemoaning a loss, "Look, kid. They don't put Ws and Ls on your paycheck."

By the halfway point of Maxwell's second season, he was clearly the best scorer on the team with an uncanny ability to squirm inside to sink weird-looking baskets. He could contort his 6'-8" frame in ways nature never in-tended and had a knack for applying just the right amount of "English" to his shots. Neither his angle nor speed of approach seemed to matter. When Maxwell released his shot, the touch was perfect. Even when he missed, the ball tended to linger on the rim, and Max was generally the first person on the boards following up a miss. His agility, coupled with his relentlessness on the offensive boards, guaranteed many trips to the foul line.

The other critical returnee was Chris Ford, a 6'-5" guard with the body of an accountant and the brain of a coach. The Celtics had plucked him away from the Detroit Pistons a year earlier (for college-star, pro-bust Earl Tatum). Then a veteran of six years, Ford had established a reputation as a heads-up guard who could play excellent team defense as well as hit the outside shot when necessary. He might have been an underdog in a 50-yard dash with a tortoise, but he had the ability to be in the right place at the right time.

Fitch knew exactly what he wanted to do with the team. He had studied the previous year's videotapes exhaustively and concluded that the Celtics had forgotten how to play NBA defense. Particularly appalling was Maxwell, who had entered the league with poor defensive fundamentals and hadn't bothered to improve them any during his first two seasons. Archibald had never been a defensive force, and Bird's defensive abilities were unknown.

Fitch established his plan from the start, and the team responded. When the season began after a tough training camp, the Celtics began winning again—and didn't stop. Opponents who had just gotten used to the idea that the Celtics were a fallen

Sidney Wicks and Curtis Rowe on the Celtics bench. The great UCLA stars had checkered pro careers, and never fulfilled the hopes that brought them to Boston.

Bird zeroes in on
the basket.

giant were assaulted by a new band of Celtics running and defending and crashing the boards. The Boston Garden, a sleepy place for two seasons, had reawakened.

The fans, of course, fell in love with Bird immediately. His numbers weren't what they would one day be, but they were good enough. And they didn't really tell the story. He was not only a scorer, but a wondrous passer. He made look-away passes, over-the-shoulder passes, touch passes, behind-the-back passes, 50-foot outlet passes, 80-foot baseball passes and all sorts of bounce passes. Cowens and his backup, Rick Robey, appreciated Bird's crisp, timely entry passes. Bird delivered the ball only when the intended recipient was ready and in the best position to take his shot.

Fitch nicknamed him "Kodak," saying that Bird took a mental picture while moving upcourt and knew where each of the other nine players were on the floor. Fitch could also have called him "IBM," because Bird could then instantly calculate the various possibilities and determine the best next move. When all else failed, Bird was even capable of passing to himself. On one occasion, when trapped inside, he threw the ball off the glass and retrieved his own miss for an easy lay-up.

At 6'-9", Bird could do many of the things Bob Cousy had done at 6'-1". Passing was just one of Bird's skills. He was a much better rebounder than the Celtics had expected, and no one had suspected how physically tough he was. Opponents quickly learned that for every elbow they delivered, they could expect two in return.

Bird was hired as a scorer, but his offensive game proved to be far more versatile than that label indicated. His jump shot was textbook perfect, his range was astounding (an increasingly significant wrinkle with the addition of the three-point shot in his rookie season), and he was equally comfortable facing the basket or playing with his back to it. Fouling him was a waste of time, because he arrived an 85 percent foul-shooter and developed into a 90 percent shooter and three-time league leader.

Most of all, Bird lived to play the game, and never stopped trying to improve his performance. His work habits soon became the stuff of legend. Celtics fans were agog. So often in life, folks are led to believe that something will be extraordinary, only to have it turn out to be quite ordinary. Bird was just the opposite. He surpassed his advanced billing. He had to. How else could a team that had lost to a bad Detroit Pistons club 160 to 117 the year before win 61 games and capture the Atlantic Division title the next year?

8 THE FITCH FACTOR

Bill Fitch orchestrates during a time-out. He has the second-best regular season winning percentage among Celtics coaches, trailing only K.C. Jones.

THE 1979-80 VERSION OF THE CELTics was a very small team. Cowens had spent his career battling bigger men, but the 6'-8", 6'-8", 6'-9" front line backed up by a 6'-5" sixth man was Lilliputian by NBA standards. The only real size was backup center Rick Robey, the product of another superb Auerbach heist. The good-natured Robey had been obtained late the previous season from Indiana for Billy Knight, a 6'-6" shooter who gave new meaning to the word "soft" when it came to putting his body on the line. The Boston Garden fans knew it and booed Knight's every move, which could account for the fact that all but one of his thirteen 20-point efforts came on the road.

Robey was more Boston's style. The 6'-11" former Kentucky Wildcat loved contact and had an accomplished inside game to boot. He had been a starter on Kentucky's 1978 NCAA championship team, and Auerbach believed that it helped to have people in the locker room who knew what winning was all about. Robey had one other thing to recommend him: he was a friend of Larry Bird. The two had met during their college days and were simpatico. Each liked to play and play hard — and each liked to really unwind after the game. They became roommates on the road, and Robey proved invaluable to Bird. Larry was slowly acclimating himself to the rigors of the

NBA and the demands of the public and the media, and he was lucky to have Robey there to run interference.

The team took no time to get rolling, and reversed the previous year's 3–12 start. Cowens was playing his best basketball since his self-imposed exile three years earlier and would make the All-Star Game for the final time in his career. Maxwell had added defense to his renowned inside scoring game; he had always been a clever passer, and demonstrated it when Bird sparked a revival in team passing. Carr was proving to be an ideal sixth man. M.L. might shake up the game with a jump shot, a drive, a steal, or even by running at the opponent's best player and making a face at him; he'd do anything to win. Ford, a solid team player who knew his own limitations, was elevated by the level of Boston's play.

But the real surprise was Archibald. His career had seemingly been ended by injury, and in two seasons from 1976 to 1978 he played in just 34 games. His absence was a loss for fans of the game, for he had been a unique offensive force. The Bronx native had run a patterned offense in college for Don Haskins at the University of Texas at El Paso. Cincinnati coach Bob Cousy was desperately seeking someone to run his offense, and picked Archibald in the second round of the 1970 NBA draft. By Archibald's third year in the league, Cousy had turned over the offense to him, and the 6'-1" guard was a terror. That year Tiny became the only player to lead the league in both scoring (34 points a game) and assists (11.4 a game). He sustained his first Achilles tendon injury when he was accidentally stepped on by seven-foot, 250-pound Chicago

Rick Robey seizes a rebound in front of Tiny Archibald.

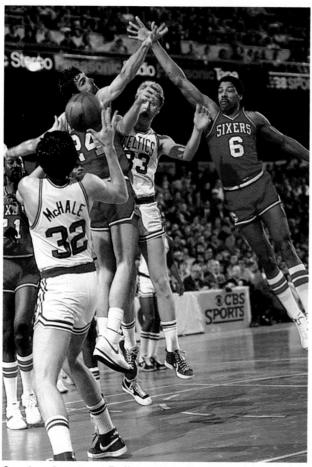

Somehow, Larry Bird slips the ball to Kevin McHale under the arms of Julius Erving and Bobby Jones of Philadelphia. Bird has proved to be the greatest passing forward the game has seen.

Despite his successes early in his career, Archibald had never been a true team leader. He had been a penetrator, a slasher, a leave-his-feet-and-see-what-happens kind of point guard. Fitch wanted Archibald to be more than that. He wanted him to be a point guard by Bob Cousy's old standard: "When a guard crosses midcourt, is he thinking pass or is he thinking shot?" says The Cooz. "If he's thinking pass, he's a point guard. If he's thinking shot, he isn't." The 1979-80 season was the first one in which Tiny Archibald would pass the Cousy point-guard test.

Not that Archibald stopped scoring — when opponents sagged on him he gladly stuck the 17-foot jumper. If he came down on the fast break and opponents played the pass, he took it to the basket with as much authority as any little man who ever played the game — with either the left hand or the right. But he would have done his job if he hadn't scored at all, because his first task was to push the ball upcourt as quickly as possible. The operative label for someone who advances the ball quickly is "push man." Tiny was a push man's push man.

The season was a joyride as the Celtics delighted in payback for the indignities of the previous two seasons. Opponents had taken special delight in thrashing the once powerful men in green. One particularly delicious evening of revenge occurred in Pontiac, Michigan. The Pistons, led by their swaggering point guard Kevin Porter, had humiliated the Celtics the previous season by scoring 160 points and winning by 43, as Coach Vitale led the cheers, waving a towel to ignite the

Bulls center Tom Boerwinkle, but came back to contribute two more outstanding seasons before being injured again.

By the time Archibald arrived in Boston in the fall of 1978, he was with his fourth team in five seasons, and not a happy man. He was overweight, sluggish, moody, and as uncertain as everyone else about his basketball future. But Fitch went out of his way to make Archibald feel wanted. Tiny arrived at training camp for his second Celtics season in good shape, and was delighted to discover a different aura surrounding the club. Fitch told him the team was a brand new car and that he was giving Tiny the keys.

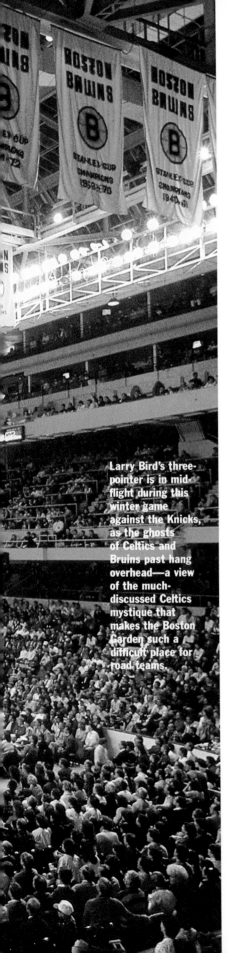

Larry Bird's three-pointer is in mid-flight during this winter game against the Knicks, as the ghosts of Celtics and Bruins past hang overhead—a view of the much-discussed Celtics mystique that makes the Boston Garden such a difficult place for road teams.

fans. On this occasion, the Pistons led by 15 at the end of three quarters. But Robey led a fourth-quarter surge, and the Celtics cut the lead to three and had the ball with seconds to go.

Fitch decided to surprise Detroit by having Cowens drift out for a three-point attempt. It bounced off the rim, but both Carr and Bird were there for the rebound. The ever-alert Carr ripped the ball away from his startled teammate, dribbled to the left corner, turned and fired a three-pointer that swished through at the buzzer. Bird later admitted that he would have instinctively laid the ball in. The Celtics won the game in overtime. Even the normally impassive Archibald was squealing with delight as he dribbled out the clock.

The three-point shot turned into a formidable weapon for the Celtics. Ford actually scored the first one in NBA history, but it took Boston until about Thanksgiving to really harness the new shot. One evening in Atlanta, Ford broke open a close game by sinking a pair of three-point bombs. The first salvaged a broken play, but the second was by design. Boston opted to spring Ford loose behind a deep pick for the shot; from then on, Ford, the designated three-point shooter, was a changed man.

The new rule was made for him, because his favorite weapon was an old-fashioned one-hand set shot straight out of a Hank Luisetti highlight film. Ford had taken set shots all through high school and college, but nobody had really paid much attention to his range. When the three-point rule came along, everybody discovered that Chris had been shooting three-pointers all along.

Of course, Ford didn't have the shot all to himself. Bird hadn't thought much about the new rule when the season began because he wasn't that sure of his range, nor interested in attracting undue attention. As a rookie, he had very strong feelings about team propriety and didn't want to upstage the veterans. It wasn't his team; it was Dave Cowens' team. When the time came for a big shot, Cowens should be the first option. In Bird's first season, he took just one do-or-die end-of-game shot — a winner off an inbounds play in Houston.

Bird finished his rookie year averaging 21 points and 10 rebounds a game, leading the team in scoring and rebounds, and ranked second in assists and steals. He played in his first All-Star Game and keyed the victory with his timely scoring, passing and rebounding. Coach Billy Cunningham had Bird on the floor in overtime and asked him to make a crucial inbounds pass from the sidelines. Bird delivered a frozen-rope pass to Moses Malone for an easy basket. He topped off his All-Star debut with the first three-point basket in the game's history.

Bird was named Rookie of the Year almost unanimously, and a first-team NBA All-Star. He walked off with everything he wanted as a rookie except what he wanted most — a championship ring.

The Celtics had no trouble with Houston (then in their conference) in the opening round of the playoffs, sweeping the Rockets in four games by an average margin of more than 18 points. But Boston fans weren't ready for the comeuppance about to be delivered by the Philadelphia 76ers.

Boston-Philadelphia was the NBA's classic rivalry. The teams had been charter members of the NBA's forerunner, the Basketball Association of America, and they were custodians of a disproportionate amount of league tradition. The rivalry reached its peak in the mid-1960s, when Bill Russell and Wilt Chamberlain led their teams into playoff battles for four successive years. Staunch fans of both clubs cherished nothing more than a victory over the other.

The Celtics lost their home-court advantage in Game One, 96 to 93. Cunningham had come up with something of a Bird deterrent, rotating two talented defensive players by the name of Jones, seven-foot Caldwell and 6'-9" Bobby. As talented as he was, Bird was

Bobby Jones gave Bird as much defensive trouble as anyone.

still a rookie, and he failed to make the adjustments for which he could be counted on later in his career. Boston won Game Two in the Garden, but Philly then won three straight. It had been too much to hope for in just one year; the fourteenth championship would have to wait.

But the wait turned out to be a short one—just one year, two weeks and three days after the disappointing loss to Philadelphia. Considering that only two years before the Celtics had been embarrassed and embarrassing, it seemed like no time at all.

After the 1980 playoffs, Bill Fitch had taken a dispassionate look at his team and concluded that it had to be bigger to get by the 76ers, let alone the world champion Lakers with ageless Kareem Abdul-Jabbar. He and Auerbach therefore worked a draft-day extravaganza, dealing the first and thirteenth selections in the draft to the Golden State Warriors for the third pick and four-year veteran Robert Parish, a seven-foot center with untapped potential. The draft pick brought in the University of Minnesota's Kevin McHale, a 6'-10" forward whose long arms made him the equivalent of a 7'-4" center. The deal improved the Celtics immeasurably without giving up anyone on the roster. In one day, the Celtics had gone from too small to big.

Fitch had long dreamed about working with Parish, who was generally regarded as an underachiever with Golden State. He possessed an excellent turnaround jumper, but what Fitch liked most about Parish was that he could run, an aspect of his game that had been neglected. Parish got all the running he would ever want at Fitch's training camp; a few days into camp, Parish had the look of a man who wished his parents had never met. That feeling intensified when Dave Cowens shocked everyone by retiring the day of an exhibition game in Indiana. Cowens was having trouble

Parish's well-known spin move, here executed against Bob Lanier, is hard to stop because he is so quick.

with his feet and legs and felt he could no longer perform up to his standards. His last official act as a Celtic was to climb onto the team bus and inform Parish that he was confident the newcomer could do the job.

Cowens might have been the only one who was confident after Parish's shaky performance that night against the Chicago Bulls. He picked up five fouls in the first quarter, but Fitch kept him in the game. The message was clear: "You're it, buddy."

Parish survived and became one of the NBA's preeminent centers. He may be the single most underrated Celtic of all time — perhaps inevitable on a franchise blessed with centers such as Russell and Cowens. Nevertheless, had Parish played for most other teams, he would have been regarded as one of the best players in the history of that club.

The other new Celtics big man achieved instant notoriety by becoming entangled in a contract hassle. McHale even flew to Italy to investigate basketball options there. But the two sides settled. Kevin flew back to the States, drove to the Celtics' practice facility at Hellenic College in suburban Brookline, Massachusetts, stepped onto the floor and embarked on one of the great NBA careers. He had "star" written all over him from the beginning. He started out blocking shots with either hand and sinking turnaround jumpers at will.

With McHale and Parish, the Celtics improved on their previous season's record, winning 62 games—the same as Philly. The two teams fought down to the final day of the season, when Boston bested the 76ers in the Garden for first place and the league's best record.

The homecourt advantage was huge, because the Celtics enjoyed unprecedented support. The Bird teams were beneficiaries of history, cheered on by third-generation fans whose fathers and grandfathers had taken them to see Cousy, Russell, Heinsohn, the Joneses and Havlicek. They knew good basketball when they saw it, and this was really good basketball. With Bird as the cornerstone and Archibald back in form, the Celtics were far and away the slickest passing team in the league. There were glorious moments when the ball would touch five pairs of hands within seconds.

After battling on virtually even terms all season, Boston and Philadelphia met in the crucial playoff contest. The series appeared headed for a repeat of Philly's 4–1 thrashing of Boston the year before, when the 76ers took a 3–1 lead and had the ball with a six-point lead and just 1:40 to play in Game Five. But the Celtics rallied to win by two, then shocked the City of Brotherly Love in Game Six by coming from 10 points down in the third quarter to tie the series.

Game Seven was one of the most emotional games in Boston Garden history. With five minutes remaining, the 76ers, led by the great Julius Erving, were up by nine points. But with the fans shrieking, the Celtics limited Philly to just one point in their final ten possessions. The score was tied with one minute to go when Darryl Dawkins wheeled in for a drive and was met by three Celtics. Fortunately, officials Darrell Garretson and Jake

The NBA was painful for Kevin McHale from the beginning.

O'Donnell had decided that day to let the boys play. Bird pulled down the rebound and dribbled upcourt. "There was nowhere else in the world I wanted the ball but in my hands," he would say later. He moved past the three-point line, bluffed a pass with his eyes and shoulders to shake off a defender, and banked an 18-footer.

The shot held up and the Celtics won, 91 to 90. Boston, which had been on the brink of elimination in Game Five, had rallied to win the final three games by point margins of two, two, and one.

The Finals were anticlimactic. The Lakers weren't there. Houston, a 40–42 regular-season team, was the western representative. The Rockets fought gamely to split the first four games. But the teams returned to Boston where Maxwell, who reveled in his reputation as a "big-game" player, came through with 28 points (on his way to a well-deserved MVP award) in a Boston rout. They went back to The Summit in Houston and finished the Rockets off by 11 on May 14, 1981.

In two years, the Celtics, to quote a well-known politician, had gone from the outhouse to the penthouse. As far as Boston's faithful following was concerned, the championship of basketball was back where it belonged.

Red Auerbach celebrates with the city's finest after the Celtics beat Philadelphia in the 1981 conference finals.

9 CELTICS PRIDE

Chief.

THE CELTICS FAILED TO DEFEND their title the next year. Philadelphia avenged its 1981 playoff loss to the Celtics by doing something it had never done before—winning a seventh game in the Boston Garden. Philly lost to the Lakers in the Finals, but the next season (1982-83) belonged to the 76ers. The team had acquired Moses Malone and was on a mission all season long; it won 65 games and stormed through the playoffs—Moses making his "Fo', Fo', Fo'" prediction of three playoff sweeps—losing just one game.

The Celtics won 56 games, but didn't manage to meet Philadelphia in the playoffs. They struggled past Atlanta in the three-game mini-series, then lost to Milwaukee in a nightmarish four straight. No Boston team had ever been dispatched like that. True, Bird had been ill, but even with him the team had been woefully ineffective.

Auerbach knew some changes had to be made, and the first was a stunner. Bill Fitch recognized that the team was no longer responding to his command and agreed to a parting of the ways. His successor was popular assistant coach K.C. Jones, the fifth former Celtics player to take the helm.

The second change was major, too. Auerbach shipped Rick Robey to Phoenix for All-Star guard Dennis Johnson. The Celtics had hoped to shore up their backcourt the previous year by acquiring former Milwaukee star Quinn Buckner, but he had been disappointing. Johnson proved to be a player with far more dimensions.

"DJ" came with a reputation. He had broken into the NBA as a second-round selection out of Pepperdine with the Seattle Supersonics back in 1976, and was the playoff MVP when Seattle won the championship in 1979. Despite his obvious talents, Johnson had a rap; word was that he was moody, selfish, uncontrollable. He was traded to Phoenix in 1980 and became a frequent All-Star as well as a perennial on the All-Defensive team. But DJ was available because Phoenix had long coveted a physical center like Rick Robey.

Johnson was an immediate hit in Boston. He brought an element of toughness and professionalism to the Celtics backcourt. Though never billed as a playmaker, he adapted quickly and well to that role, and his reputation for defensive prowess was deserved. Nobody appreciated the new Celtic more than Larry Bird. By the end of their second season together, Bird was calling DJ "the best player I've ever played with."

With Johnson, the Celtics could handle the departure of Archibald, who was waived after the 1982-83 season. DJ could adjust to any running mate and played equally comfortably alongside Buckner, Gerald Henderson

Executive vice-president and general manager Jan Volk.

Newcomer Dennis Johnson combines with Bird and McHale to stifle a Nets attempt.

or Danny Ainge, the former first-team All-American from Brigham Young University whom Auerbach had coaxed away from baseball's Toronto Blue Jays.

The 1983-84 Celtics were a devastating team, winning 62 games and the Atlantic Division by 10 games over Philly. Bird won his first of three successive MVP awards. K.C. Jones proved to be the perfect coach for this squad. He was the "cool" antidote to Fitch's heat. He motivated the team by the force of his personal dignity, not by screaming or other methods of intimidation. He recognized that the Celtics were intelligent veterans who knew how to play the game, and he let them play. He was confident enough to welcome their suggestions, but never let the team drift toward anarchy.

After defeating Washington in four playoff games, the Celtics encountered the New York Knicks, led by their irrepressible scoring machine, Bernard King. He single-handedly carried the series to seven games before Bird and the Celtics prevailed in Boston Garden. It was far easier taking revenge on Milwaukee for the previous year's sweep, and the Celtics brushed them aside in five games. That advanced Boston to the Finals and another confrontation with their rivals from yesteryear, the Lakers. The two teams had met six times for the championship, with Boston prevailing each time. But this would be their first series in 15 years, and the first high-level showdown between superstars Larry Bird and Magic Johnson since the 1979 NCAA championship game.

The Lakers will always regard this series as The One That Got Away—and rightly so. L.A. won the first game in Boston and appeared to have the second won as well. Then James Worthy hung a pass out to dry in the game's final seconds, and an alert Gerald Henderson picked it off and went in for a lay-up to tie the game. The Celtics prevailed as L.A., rattled by the turnabout, handled the ball like a bar of soap in overtime. The Lakers rebounded to win the third game at home easily. But poor ball-handling and monster efforts from Bird (29 points, 21 rebounds) and Parish sent the series back to Boston even.

There the Celtics found an ally in Mother Nature. Stifling weather drove the temperature to 97 degrees inside the ancient and unairconditioned Garden. The Lakers wilted and Bird flourished, shooting 15 of 20 to lead Boston to a big win. When they returned to Boston for the climactic game, Cedric Maxwell, who relished seventh games, told his younger teammates, "Jump on my back, boys." He then went over, under, around and through young James Worthy in a virtuoso display. Ainge came off the bench to give the Celtics a valuable second-quarter lift, and Boston cruised, 111 to 102, to its fifteenth championship.

No member of the team appreciated the triumph more than Coach Jones. As coach of the Washington Bullets in 1975, he had taken a powerful squad to the Finals, only to see his team swept by an overachieving Golden State squad. The prevailing impression was that he had been outcoached. K.C.'s departure from Washington the following season had not been pretty, and he spent the next two years in despair before old friend Satch Sanders summoned him back to Boston as an assistant coach.

DJ and Gerald
Henderson savor
the 1984 victory
over L.A. with
Brent Musberger.
Henderson was a
series hero: his
steal and layup as
time ran out tied
Game Two, which
the Celtics won in
overtime to prevent
a Lakers sweep of
the first two games
in the Garden.

K.C. Jones has the best regular season and playoff winning percentage among Celtics coaches.

DJ drives on Detroit's Joe Dumars.

K.C. remained in that position, decidedly in the background under both Dave Cowens and Bill Fitch, and it was no secret in Boston's traveling party that Fitch did not value K.C.'s counsel. K.C. himself didn't think he'd ever get another crack at a head-coaching job. Yet he proved to be precisely the answer to a discouraged team when he took over in 1983. The Celtics responded to his understated approach, and more than one player said the game had become a simple matter of trying to win for the coach. When the team knocked off L.A., the Celtics were cheering for their vindicated coach as much as for themselves.

Repeating as NBA champion is one of the most difficult challenges in professional sports. The 1984-85 Celtics were the latest in a long list of unsuccessful aspirants since the Celtics last turned the trick in 1969. Despite Bird's continued heroics and the increasing inside dominance of McHale, Los Angeles finally took a championship series from Boston, winning in six games.

The highlight of the Celtics season was a little March scoring duel. On Sunday, March 3, 1985, McHale torched the Detroit Pistons for 22 field goals and 12 free throws to establish a new Celtics single-game scoring mark of 56 points. Bird jokingly said that Kevin would have been smarter to score as many as he could, say 60. A little more than a week later, Bird demonstrated that he wasn't just making idle chitchat. Playing the Atlanta

Bird and DJ exult after the two of them stole Game Five from Detroit in the 1987 playoffs. Had the Pistons won, they would have gone home needing only one victory to get to the Finals. But Bird pilfered Isiah Thomas' inbounds toss and passed to DJ for the game-winning lay-up as time expired, stunning the Pistons and effectively saving the series.

Hawks in New Orleans, Larry erased Kevin's effort from the record books by scoring 60 points, the last on a buzzer-beating foul-line jumper. Bird was so hot that even the Atlanta bench was enthralled. In one memorable moment, Larry tossed in a downtown off-balance jumper in front of the Atlanta bench and two Atlanta subs reacted by falling off their chairs onto the floor.

Maxwell suffered through the season with a bad knee and was unavailable during the playoffs. That left the Celtics one big man shy of a full load. During the off-season, the Celtics began negotiating with Bill Walton, the brilliant but fragile center who had led the Portland Trailblazers to a championship in 1977. Since then, his career had been derailed by a series of foot ailments. In related transactions, Walton signed with the Celtics and the veteran Maxwell was dealt to the Los Angeles Clippers.

General Manager Jan Volk had one more Auerbach-like trick up his sleeve. Believing the team needed more bench production, he signed free agent Jerry Sichting, a tough little guard with a big heart and an unerring jump shot. Thus the cast was assembled for another run at the title. The starting five were All-Star Robert Parish at center, All-Stars Larry Bird and Kevin McHale at forward, All-Star Dennis Johnson and then-underrated but future All-Star Danny Ainge at guard. Bill Walton, a former All-Star, was the back-up center. Scott Wedman, a one-time All-Star who had been quietly providing important bench scoring since the Celtics acquired him in 1982 (including the winning basket in Game Two of the 1984 Finals), was the third forward. Sichting was the third guard. For further support, K.C. could count on hard-working Greg Kite to bang bodies inside and cerebral Rick Carlisle to shore up the backcourt. Athletic youngsters David Thirdkill and first-round draft pick Sam Vin-

Kevin McHale's short jump hook became as effective as any inside shot in the league.

Jerry Sichting sparked the Celtics off the bench in the championship year of 1985-86, his first with the team.

Michael Jordan *en route* to setting a playoff scoring record of 63 points in the double-overtime game on April 20, 1986 — eventually won by the Celtics.

cent completed the roster.

The team did not jell immediately. Walton had some shaky early moments, most notably a turnover-laden disaster of a performance on opening night when the Celtics blew an 18-point lead and lost in overtime in New Jersey. Bird had back and elbow problems from the start of the season, which adversely affected his shooting. But this team was talented enough to carry Larry until he healed. The turnaround came after a Christmas Day game in Madison Square Garden. Despite some more un-Birdlike marksmanship (8 of 27), Boston built up a 25-point third-quarter lead. But instead of a victory, the Celtics left New York with a humiliating double-overtime defeat.

The loss proved helpful. It triggered something inside the Celtics, who knew they were too good for such a fate. The team won its next four games, lost one, then reeled off 13 straight. Bird was feeling better, and the team was taking shape. And what a team it was. Comparing the great Boston teams is a risky enterprise, what with changing times and the evolving dynamics of sport. The early Celtics teams were both smaller and slower than their mid-1980s counterparts, and teams must be judged against their own era. Still, Celtics fans sensed that they were watching the most artistically satisfying Boston Celtics team of all time.

Somehow, more than the Russell-Cousy teams, more than the Havlicek-Cowens teams, and even more than the original Bird-Archibald team, this club seemed to be the essence of team basketball. The public responded. The Celtics had always been popular in the hinterlands, but suddenly large numbers of people began greeting the team with green T-shirts, hats and banners at airports and in hotel lobbies.

These Celtics seemed to possess every weapon. They could destroy opponents with inside power, medium-range jumpers, or three-point bombs. They harrassed defensively on the perimeter and intimidated defensively on the interior with the shot-blocking skills of Parish, McHale and Walton. But most of all, they passed the basketball. They passed it as it had never been passed before and has not been passed since. Putting Bird, the best-passing forward who has ever lived, on the floor with Walton, the best-passing center who has ever lived, was downright diabolical. The crowd began howling the moment the seven-foot

Ever alert, Bird looks to pass while on the floor, but sees only Mark Acres, who is also sitting down.

redhead got the summons from K.C. and trotted to the scorer's table. They knew the wait for at least one bring-'em-out-of-their-seats pass would be short. They believed themselves to be the luckiest 14,890 sports fans in the world to witness such a spectacle.

The Celtics steamrolled through the months of January, February, March and April. When McHale was lost for ten games due to an Achilles tendon injury, Wedman simply stepped in and scored 15 points a game. When this joyride of a season was over, the Celtics had won 67 games, their second best total ever.

The playoffs contained precious little suspense. The only hint of peril came in the final seconds of Game Two of the opening series, when Michael Jordan, on his way to a playoff record 63 points, missed an open jumper that would have won the game. The Celtics prevailed in a second overtime and settled back into cruise control. In each series, Boston won the first two games at home and breezed. Atlanta fell in five games, embarrassed when the Celtics broke open the final game with a 36 to 6 third-quarter margin. Milwaukee fell in four straight. Instead of the vaunted Lakers, the Celtics' final opponent was, as in 1981, the young, athletic Houston Rockets. As in 1981, the Celtics won in six games with Bird putting on a dazzling display of all-around basketball skill.

It had been a season to remember. The spicy extra ingredient had been Walton, who after so many disappointments had managed a rare full season of play. He suited up for 80 games, missing one with a broken nose and another due to illness. He missed neither a game nor a practice because of his foot problems. Walton's previous season high had been just 67. Big Bill and Bird developed a symbiotic athlet-

Danny Ainge always played hard, which occasionally made him the focal point of opposing fans' ire.

Bill Walton and Robert Parish controlled the boards during the 1986 playoffs, perhaps the high point of the Celtics inside game.

ic relationship. Their mutual thoughts were transformed into basketball action. Walton's very presence revived Parish, who had been playing too many minutes and was often worn out down the stretch. With Walton as the anchor, K.C. could unleash his "Green Team"—the second team, so named because it wears green in practice (the first unit wears white). Sichting and Wedman, deadly open shooters who thrived on moving without the ball, must have thought that they had died and gone to basketball heaven as Walton continually fed them the ball from the post.

Among its many achievements that season, this edition of the Celtics established the greatest homecourt dominance in league history. The only thing separating Boston from a perfect season in the Garden was one lone December setback at the hands of Portland.

Sadly, the euphoria lasted but one season. Beset by the inevitable injuries, Walton would play only 22 more games as a Celtic over the next two years. Had he remained healthy, Boston might have added a few more championships.

Even without Walton, the Celtics fought their way back to the finals in 1987, overcoming tremendous adversity to win back-to-back seven-game playoff series against Milwaukee and

Danny Ainge is surrounded by Pistons during the 1987-88 conference finals, won by Detroit.

Detroit. (The latter was made easier when, in the fourth quarter of the final game, Piston teammates Vinnie Johnson and Adrian Dantley collided violently; Johnson was slowed for the remainder of the game, and Dantley, the team's leading scorer, was rushed to the hospital.) Bird gilded his legend with a game-saving steal and feed to a cutting Dennis Johnson, who beat the buzzer with a lay-up to salvage Game Five against Detroit. But Bird could not overcome back problems, which hampered his shooting in the losing six-game effort against Los Angeles.

The aching Bird had been the healthiest of the frontcourt starters. Parish sustained one sprained ankle after another, but kept playing because the Celtics had no one to spell him. McHale, in the midst of his greatest season, suffered a broken foot in February when he was inadvertently stepped on by Phoenix forward Larry Nance. A valiant McHale played right through the last game of the playoffs on what was diagnosed as a cracked navicular bone. The resultant surgery would keep him out of the first month of the following season.

Until the injury, McHale had been redefining the concept of inside scoring. He was shooting about 60 percent from the floor with his bewildering assortment of jump hooks, finger rolls and tricky inside moves as well as his turnaround jumper. Veteran NBA observers were anointing him as the greatest inside scoring forward the league had ever seen.

The Celtics did not get as far the following season. Though they won another Atlantic Division crown (the eighth in nine years during the Bird era), a lack of bench strength placed an intolerable burden on the overworked starters. Even so, Boston outlasted the young and talented Atlanta Hawks, winning a sixth game in Atlanta to

force a dramatic seventh game at home. Bird and Atlanta star Dominique Wilkins staged an unforgettable fourth-quarter shootout. Bird shot 9 of 10 and racked up 20 of his 34 points; he needed them all to keep pace with Wilkins, who scored 15 in the final stanza and 47 in the game. The two teams shot a combined 59 percent from the floor while committing just 15 turnovers.

But Bird couldn't get it going in the conference final against Detroit, and the Celtics fell in six games. Boston fans could only wonder what a healthy Bill Walton or a young Lenny Bias would have done to relieve the overworked frontcourt. (Bias, Boston's top 1987 draft pick and the second selection in the entire draft, died of a cocaine overdose only a few hours after becoming a Celtic.) Los Angeles bested Detroit in an exciting seven-game championship series to successfully defend its title, the first team to do so since Bill Russell's swan song in 1969.

10 ONCE AND FUTURE KINGS

Second-year forward Reggie Lewis blossomed into a star in Bird's absence, averaging more than 20 points per game as a starter. Here, he slips by Philadelphia's Hersey Hawkins for a jumper in the lane.

THE 1988-89 SEASON WAS ONE OF transition. That had been signaled the previous season, when the Celtics announced that K.C. Jones would retire from coaching and move into the front office, and assistant coach Jimmy Rodgers would take up the reins of the ball club. K.C. had guided the team to two championships and had proved to be the perfect coach for a veteran club. However, during the previous two campaigns, he had shown little faith in or patience with his bench. As a result, the starters — particularly the frontcourt of Robert Parish, Kevin McHale and Larry Bird — were forced to play too many minutes and were battered and exhausted by the time the playoffs came around. Moreover, no bench had been developed, and no relief was in sight.

In his very first regular-season game as coach, Rodgers signaled that his approach would be different from K.C.'s. He surprised the Garden regu-

lars by replacing veteran starter Danny Ainge with rookie Brian Shaw for the fourth-quarter stretch. Shaw played the rest of the way and helped trigger a rally, as the Celtics bested the New York Knicks in overtime.

It was clear the bench would, for better or worse, get more playing time, and that soon became a necessity. After just six games in which Bird was hampered by his troublesome Achilles tendons, the superstar opted for surgery on both his heels and was, it turned out, lost for the season.

Without their anchor, the Celtics foundered. Despite some great efforts by the veterans — particularly center Robert Parish, who was downright ma-

K. C. Jones, Red Auerbach, and Jan Volk with current owners Don F. Gaston, Paul R. Dupee, Jr., and Alan N. Cohen.

Rookie guard Brian Shaw started much of the 1988–89 season. However, he only had a one-year contract, and over the summer he shocked the team and its fans by signing a multimillion-dollar deal to play in Italy.

jestic (third in the league in rebounding and field-goal percentage) — the Birdless Celtics were decidedly ordinary. Even though Boston was still tough at home in the Garden, the team was dismal on the road. It failed to win back-to-back road games for the first time in 40 years. Its 10 road victories came at the expense of the worst teams in the NBA; on the road against teams with a winning record, the Celtics didn't win a single game in 23 tries. Boston needed a hard-fought win at home against the expansion Charlotte Hornets to finish just above .500 (42–40, by far the worst record of the Bird era) and capture the final playoff spot in the Eastern Conference.

Celtics fans had gone into the season hoping for a rematch with the Detroit Pistons. But they had envisioned that showdown in the conference finals, not in the very first round. The Pistons, as expected, had developed into the league powerhouse, and they quickly dispatched Boston in three straight games en route to their first NBA championship. It was the first time since 1956 (pre–Bill Russell) that the Celtics had made the playoffs and lost in the first round.

However, Boston's quick exit from the playoffs and mediocre record don't tell the full story of the 1988-89 season. In one year, the team underwent a dramatic makeover. Only seven of the 15 players with the Celtics when the season ended had been with the club the previous year. You truly needed a program to recognize the men in green and white. The Boston front office pursued every avenue — the draft, a major trade, and the Continental Basketball Association — to infuse the club with a couple of elements that had been almost completely absent: youth and speed.

The most important new contributors arrived via the draft. Thanks to their on-court success, the Celtics had been drafting low in the first round for

High above the floor, Kareem and Robert Parish entwine.

years—and without much luck. College stars like Michigan State's Sam Vincent and University of Houston's Michael Young came to Boston with great college records, yet couldn't contribute with the Celtics. But in 1987 and 1988, the Celtics came up with back-to-back gems: 6'-7" swingman Reggie Lewis, who had set scoring records at Northeastern University, and 6'-6" guard Brian Shaw out of the University of California at Santa Barbara.

Lewis brought one of the quickest first steps seen in a Celtics uniform in years. He could drive, and he could stop on a dime for crisp, 15-foot jumpers. Reggie wasn't afraid to put it up. Inserted into the starting lineup when Bird went out, Lewis led the team in field-goal attempts. He proved to be the first Celtic since Charlie Scott able to create his own shot without benefit of a pick. Thanks to Lewis' athleticism, Boston fans were treated to some spectacular jams, a basketball staple for years on virtually every team but the Celtics.

The point guard role was gradually transferred from Dennis Johnson to Shaw, who reminded many observers of a young DJ. With his height and long arms, Brian played tenacious defense and was a force on the boards. While the youngster had trouble hitting the jumper consistently, he improved steadily throughout the year and was very effective when he drove to the basket. His talents were on particular display in the short playoff series against Detroit.

Ed Pinckney drives against the Nets' Buck Williams. Pinckney was part of the Ainge and Lohaus for Kleine and Pinckney trade with Sacramento, which helped overhaul the Celtics roster.

The infusion of young legs helped, but it was not enough. With Bird out of the lineup, there was too much of a burden on Parish and McHale. They were playing too many minutes and weakening late in the game; the Celtics lost a string of games down the fourth-quarter stretch, the kind of close games the team had always counted on winning. In mid-season, the team completed its biggest trade since it had landed Dennis Johnson some seven years before.

The bait was Danny Ainge. By dint of hard work and hustle, Ainge had turned himself into an All-Star guard. He was one of the best long-range shooters in the game, having set a league record for three-pointers the year before. (Without Ainge and Bird, the Celtics ranked last in the league in three-pointers.) Boston sent Ainge and second-year player Brad Lohaus, a seven-footer with potential for which the Celtics could no longer afford to wait, to the Sacramento Kings; in return, they got some inside relief—forward Ed Pinckney, a 6'-9" leaper, and center Joe Kleine, a 6'-11" banger.

Both Pinckney and Kleine were young veterans. Both had been high first-round draft choices four years before. Neither had distinguished himself in the pro ranks. Pinckney had made contributions off the bench in both Phoenix and Sacramento, while Kleine had settled into a backup role with the Kings. But the Celtics hoped that the two, surrounded by better talent and called upon to be classic Celtics role players, would respond to a new challenge. They made an immediate impact in their new uniforms, yet were erratic as the team stumbled down the stretch. But their potential was obvious for all to see.

The final resource for the Celtics was the Continental Basketball Association. Once strictly a run-and-gun league of lost dreams, the CBA has evolved into something of a genuine

minor league. NBA stars like the Denver Nuggets' Michael Adams have done stints in the CBA and successfully returned to the big league. With Ainge sacrificed to shore up the frontcourt, the Celtics badly needed backcourt help. They signed two CBA guards— 6'-5" Kevin Gamble, the league's leading scorer, and 6'-2" Kelvin Upshaw, a playmaker who had started the season with the Miami Heat.

Gamble had great difficulty adjusting to the Celtics attack and looked like a sure candidate for the inactive list when Bird returned for the playoffs. But a few games before the end of the season, Dennis Johnson injured his ankle. Gamble was inserted into the starting lineup. For the final six games, the former Iowa star displayed

The 1988–89 season was a year of frustration for Larry Bird. Sidelined after six games by heel surgery, he attended most home games and was a regular presence at the end of the Celtics bench.

Parish was magnificent during the 1988-89 season as he tried to make up for Bird's absence.

the scoring touch that had been so evident in the CBA; he averaged 23 points a game, scoring frequently with slashing drives to the hoop and thunderous dunks.

Upshaw was an immediate hit. He was the perfect push-up man for the second unit, blending speed with control. He dished out assists neatly and hit the medium-range jumper often enough to keep the defense honest.

The six new youngsters weren't enough to salvage the season. And no one could say for sure that all would have successful NBA careers. But they were promising enough to have the team and its fans looking to the future with renewed hope. The Celtics had gone into the 1988-89 season as an aging aggregation (all five starters were over 30) with no prospects beyond the immediate future. Now they had a young and talented corps of players to bolster the aging stars.

History has taught the people of Boston that the wait for the proud Celtics tradition to continue is never a long one. Continuity is the team's hallmark. It separates the Celtics from all other franchises. Rock music may blare from loudspeakers in other arenas, but Garden fans are soothed by an organist who plays only when it's appropriate. A parquet floor was good enough for Bob Cousy, and now it's good enough for Brian Shaw. The famous flags overhead are a testament — like no others in sport — to those who have gone before. Red Auerbach still sits in his midcourt seat, his mind focused on the future; leave the reminiscing to the writers and the fans.

No glittering new arena will ever quite match the atmosphere of the old Boston Garden. The emphasis here has always been on the game, first and foremost. And the best basketball ever seen anywhere has been played in Boston. There is every reason to expect that it will be again.

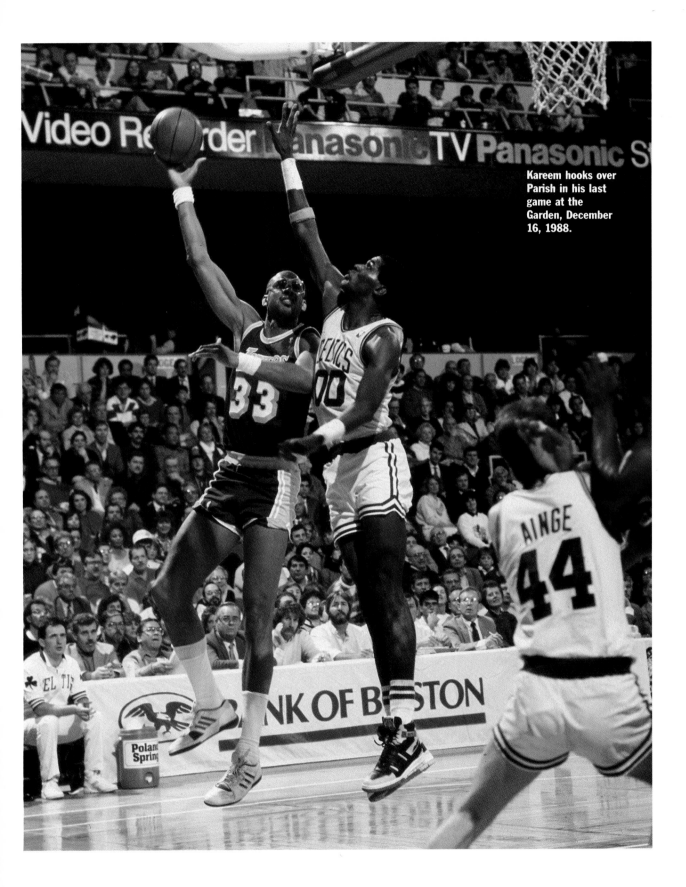

Kareem hooks over Parish in his last game at the Garden, December 16, 1988.

11COACHES

Tom Heinsohn.

From John
"Honey" Russell to
Jimmy Rodgers, the
Celtics have had
ten coaches, and
nowhere is the
team's family
tradition more
evident: five have
been former
players, and one
(Rodgers) was a
long-time assistant
before becoming
head coach.
Though varying
greatly in style and
success, the ten
coaches have
collectively led
the Celtics to a
remarkable
regular-season
mark of
2,115–1,198 (a
.638 winning
percentage), and a
playoff record of
257–170 (.601),
from 1946–47
through 1988–89.
Clockwise from
left: Bill Russell,
Dave Cowens, Bill
Fitch, Jimmy
Rodgers, and
K.C. Jones.

Even after his career on the bench was over, Red Auerbach sometimes couldn't restrain himself. Here, incensed at his behavior, Red assaults Philadelphia coach Billy Cunningham during a preseason game as Sixers Moe Cheeks, Andrew Toney and others look on in astonishment.

Tom Heinsohn.

Tom Sanders.

12 RETIRED NUMBERS

A gathering of
Celtics greats from
yesteryear, with the
man who coached
them all. From left:
Cousy, Havlicek,
Auerbach, Ramsey,
Sam Jones, and
Heinsohn.

THE PANTHEON. NO TEAM HAS created the aura of continuity through the retirement of numbers more successfully than Boston. The Celtics have retired 15 numbers and one nickname. Some say they have retired too many numbers — that they have elevated the merely good into a rather rarified atmosphere by hoisting the numbers of players with relatively modest career accomplishments. That may be a good statistical argument, but the Celtics have never been about stats. They have been about winning and about sacrifice and, in the final analysis, about honor. Would any other team have retired "Loscy" to honor Jim Loscutoff? Probably not. That's why, when it comes to tradition in basketball, there are the Boston Celtics and there is everyone else.

#1 — Walter Brown

No Boston Celtic ever wore number one, and now none ever will. It was retired out of respect to the club's founder, Walter Brown, a man who personified the term "sportsman." His word was his bond, and his love of the Celtics was pure.

#2 — Red Auerbach

This honorary designation was a tribute to Red Auerbach, the embodiment of the Boston Celtics. As coach for 16 seasons and head of the front-office brain trust since 1950, he has presided over the enterprise with feistiness, intelligence and unparalleled skill. He was the greatest coach in NBA history and the true architect of the Celtics success story.

#6 — Bill Russell

Russell's 11 championship rings in 13
seasons as a player (two out of three as
Celtics coach) say it all. The greatest
individual defensive player and clutch
rebounder the game has ever known,
Russ saved his best performances for
the big games. No one knew how to win
better than Bill Russell.

#10 — Jo Jo White

A superb jump shooter and underrated
playmaker, Jo Jo White was a source of
scoring consistency on the great Celtics teams of the early and mid-1970s.
White transformed his walk-up college
game to power Boston's fast-breaking
attack.

#14 — Bob Cousy

The franchise wouldn't have made it to the glory days had it not been for Bob Cousy's magnetism and box-office appeal. "The Cooz" wrote the book for all future point guards. He still stands as the greatest ball handler and middle man on the fast break the game has ever seen.

#15 — Tom Heinsohn

"Tommy Gun" loved to shoot, but there was far more to his game than an assortment of running hooks and line-drive jumpers. He was an excellent rebounder, making a science of the offensive boards, and one tough cookie to boot. Tom Heinsohn also proved to be a student of the whole game in his tenure as coach.

#16 — Tom Sanders

The premier defensive forward of his day and a classic Auerbach role player. "Satch" was tough inside and a good rebounder, but his main task was to shut down the other team's high-scoring forward.

#17 — John Havlicek

"Hondo" was Mr. Perpetual Motion—he started running in his first training scrimmage and didn't stop until his final 29-point game 16 years later. There has never been a player with more stamina than John Havlicek—and none who could beat you in so many different ways.

#18 — Dave Cowens

The big redhead starred on two championship teams and won himself a league MVP award in 1972-73. Dave Cowens was a ferocious rebounder and relentless runner who stared down every bigger center and beat up every smaller one.

#19 — Don Nelson

Don Nelson still ranks as Auerbach's greatest bargain. Red picked him off the waiver wire in 1965 and he stayed through 11 seasons. Nelson was a deadly jump shooter who led the league in field-goal percentage at age 34. At critical moments, the Celtics would call time-out and run play 14 for "Nellie."

#21 — Bill Sharman

Bill Sharman was the premier shooter of the 1950s, impeccable at the foul line. The fans never knew how much respect he earned as a defensive guard. Sharman's devotion to physical conditioning put him some 20 years ahead of his time.

#22 — Ed Macauley

"Easy Ed" was a skinny guy who could really shoot, and, along with Cousy and Sharman, formed the mainstay of the pre-Russell era. He lacked muscle inside, but could shoot with any center of his day. His confrontations with the great George Mikan of the Minneapolis Lakers (above) set the stage for the epic pivot rivalries to come. Still, his biggest contribution to the Celtics was acting as the trade bait that brought Russell to Boston.

#23 — Frank Ramsey

The first of Auerbach's storied sixth men, Frank Ramsey had a knack for coming in cold off the bench and hitting a couple of shots. He added speed and intelligence to the attack, then taught Havlicek how to replace him before retiring.

#24 — Sam Jones

Sam boasted a killer first step and was a master of the glass. He was the best clutch shooter of the Russell teams. Though sometimes overshadowed by bigger-name players, he earned immense respect from those who know the game. Sam Jones was named a member of the NBA's silver anniversary team in 1971.

#25 — K.C. Jones

When K.C. Jones attached himself to a rival guard, that man was in for a long night's work. K.C. succeeded Cousy as team quarterback, but, like his buddy Satch Sanders, his greatest minutes were played out on the defensive end of the floor.

LOSCY — Jim Loscutoff

"Jungle Jim" had his nickname retired because his number, 18, had already been raised to the rafters for Cowens. Loscy was a ferocious rebounder and competitor who did all the dirty work for the Celtics' first great teams. Auerbach and his teammates loved him for it.

13 ROLE PLAYERS

Don Chaney played the consummate supporting role on Celtics teams of the early 1970s.

N O BASKETBALL TEAM IN HISTORY has paid as much attention to the "role player" — the significant athlete who is not a star and often not a starter, but who still makes a key contribution to the team. The Celtics have always recognized that their brilliant soloists must be backed by competent ensemble players. Some of these players developed major followings among Boston Garden fans. Some of the most beloved Celtics never saw an All-Star Game except on television.

Gene Conley

No Celtic ever had a stranger career than Gene Conley. Of course, no Celtic ever began his career in 1952-53 and played his second season six years later after, among other things, having been the winning pitcher in a major-league baseball All-Star Game (1955). This superb two-sport athlete walked back into the NBA and became the perfect backup to Bill Russell. The 6′-

8″ Conley would arrive when the Red Sox season was over and head back to the pitcher's mound after the Celtics had wrapped up another championship. He was a solid rebounder, a good team player and, teammates say, as good a fighter as the Celtics have ever put on the floor.

Larry Siegfried

"Siggy" came to the Celtics after the American Basketball Association folded, and he stayed for seven productive seasons. "Siggy's in his shirt" became Johnny Most's nightly radio call as John Havlicek's former Ohio State teammate latched onto an opponent on defense and never let the poor man out of his grasp. Siegfried came to personify the essence of a True Celtic. He dove for every loose ball and demanded nothing less than 100 percent

hustle from his teammates. He had good, though not great, scoring and playmaking skills. But his real value could not be measured in points or assists, and the fans loved him for his feisty on-court personality.

Mel Counts

As the 1964 number-one draft choice, Mel Counts was a disappointment. He stayed only two years before being traded for veteran Bailey Howell. But Counts will always be remembered as the first seven-footer to use the jump shot as his basic weapon. That's right, Brad Sellers and Brad Lohaus — Mel Counts is your spiritual forefather.

Don Chaney

With his long arms and upper body, Don Chaney established himself as a rugged defender and a legitimate heir to K.C. Jones' role as defensive stopper from the guard position. Chaney worked ceaselessly on his shot in order to make himself an offensive threat, and became a dangerous man in the Celtics' running offense of the early 1970s. He jumped to the American Basketball Association in 1975, but two years later returned via a trade with the Lakers and stayed for three more seasons. "The Duck" played with quiet dignity and will long be remembered as one of the most dedicated of the Celtics.

Art Williams

When Tommy Heinsohn wanted to take his offense up-tempo, say from 45 to 78 RPM, he called on Art "Hambone" Williams, one of the original push-up guards. Acquired before the 1969-70 season from San Diego, the veteran proved to be an ideal third guard. Havlicek loved playing with him on offense because he really delivered the ball to the open man. On defense, Williams was a scrapper who would switch onto anybody and could box much bigger men off the boards.

Henry Finkel

"High Henry" Finkel drew the toughest assignment ever — succeeding Bill Russell in 1969. When Dave Cowens arrived in 1970, this amiable seven-footer settled into a backup role, for which he was better suited. For five more seasons he set picks, blocked out on the boards, and tossed up his array of soft hooks and stationary set shots, while working hard on defense every second he was on the court. Off the court, he kept the team loose with his wisecracks. The fans didn't always appreciate Finkel, but his coach and teammates did.

Steve Kuberski

There was nothing fancy about Steve Kuberski. The 6'-8" forward took his jump shot, got his rebounds, and never tried to finesse anybody. During the 1972 Eastern Conference semifinals, Kuberski played his series of a lifetime with three 20-plus games in the six-game conquest of Atlanta. He never played as well before or after, but he was steady off the bench for more than seven seasons (surrounding a two-year expansion stint).

Rick Robey

Rick Robey provided solid and occasionally brilliant pivot play for five seasons before being traded to Phoenix for Dennis Johnson. Robey had two great strengths—he was totally ambidextrous inside, and he loved to run the floor, which helped him score on a lot of sneak-away dunks. He put in his most productive years before Kevin McHale arrived and cut into his playing time. When Cowens was hurt in 1980, Robey filled in and shot over 70 percent for the month. If he had paid a little more attention to conditioning, Robey's NBA career might have been a lot longer and brighter.

Chris Ford.

Chris Ford

Chris Ford survived a decade in the NBA on guile and a nice long-range shot. He joined the Celtics late in his career and fit perfectly into the team rebuilt around Larry Bird. Ford hit the first three-pointer in league history against Houston in 1979, and was the first NBA player to use the shot as a weapon. Despite lacking quickness, he played good, heady team defense.

Gerald Henderson

Gerald Henderson will be remembered first and foremost for the steal and driving lay-up that saved Game Two of the 1984 Finals against L.A. But there was more to his five-year stint in Boston than one heads-up play. He was an integral part of Boston's backcourt, playing either point- or off-guard. His tenacity was a critical weapon in the team's defensive arsenal.

Gerald Henderson.

M.L. Carr

M.L. Carr joined the Celtics as a free agent in 1979 and fit into the sixth-man slot immediately. Though he was later dogged by injuries, he made significant contributions over the next five seasons. His aggressive defense made him a feared player around the league, and he was always a Garden favorite—Carr could whip the crowd into a frenzy with one wave of the towel. He established himself as the conscience of the team; self-sacrifice was all but mandatory as long as M.L. was around.

M.L. Carr.

14 SIXTH MEN

A classic Havlicek leaner, always in control, splitting between Pistons Bob Lanier and Chris Ford.

AUERBACH'S CELTICS DID NOT IN-vent the concept of the sixth man, but no team has done more to popularize, even glamorize, the job. The classic sixth man, according to Auerbach, strengthens the team by his very presence. He has been chosen to start on the bench because of his ability to play more than one position or help the team in more than one way. The sixth spot is an emotional role, and the player filling it has to be able to deliver immediately without benefit of warm-up. Such stars as Frank Ramsey, John Havlicek, Paul Silas, Kevin McHale and Bill Walton have all presented their interpretations of the role for Boston.

John Havlicek.

Frank Ramsey

The old "Kentucky Colonel" was the original Celtics sixth man and wrote the book on the job. Ramsey could handle more than one position and affect the game in numerous ways. Though just 6'-3", he was tough enough and clever enough to play forward. Auerbach reasoned that bigger forwards would have more difficulty keeping up with Ramsey than Frank would have handling them (with Bill Russell as a defensive safety, of course). And when Ramsey played guard, he was a real big guard for the era. He had an incredible capacity to come in cold and hit his first shot. It seldom took him long to get his name on the stat sheet.

John Havlicek

Unquestionably the greatest two-position player ever, John Havlicek did more to glamorize the role of sixth man than anyone ever has. He provided coaches Auerbach and Russell with quality play off the bench as both forward and guard for seven seasons. When Heinsohn took over as coach, Havlicek became a starter and elevated his game even further. His mentor, Ramsey, taught him various tricks of the trade, such as keeping his warm-up pants and jacket unsnapped so he could fling them off when sent into the game. Eventually, Hondo surpassed his teacher in the sixth-man role.

Paul Silas

Coach Heinsohn had to sell the sixth-man job to Silas. When he arrived in Boston, Silas was 29 and felt he deserved to be a starter. But Silas put a new spin on the position. Whereas Ramsey and Havlicek had been scorers first, Silas' forte was rebounding. He would come into a game and change it with a power rebound or two, a sneaky elbow in the ribs, or a tip-in on the offensive boards. The Garden crowd tuned in to his particular brand of ball immediately, which, in turn, generated enthusiasm in Silas for his role.

Kevin McHale

Kevin McHale was the first rookie since Havlicek 18 years before him to be handed the juicy sixth-man role. But McHale never seemed like a rookie. He was uncommonly poised and simply put on his uniform that first day and began knocking in turnaround jumpers, burying hook shots, blocking shots with either hand and hauling in rebounds. He was a devastating weapon off the bench and combined with Larry Bird, Robert Parish, Cedric Maxwell and M.L. Carr to give the Celtics one of the great frontcourts in NBA history. McHale enjoyed his sixth-man slot for four years until Maxwell departed, then quickly proved himself to be the finest inside-scoring forward in NBA history.

Bill Walton

For one glorious season, the man who once appeared destined to rank among the best two or three centers in NBA history had to settle for being the best sixth man in basketball. It was all right with him. Bill Walton combined with Robert Parish to give Boston 48 minutes of All-Star caliber play in the pivot. As the 1985-86 season progressed, the two became a Boston version of the Twin Towers and, on those occasions when they were paired, totally dominated the boards. Walton and Larry Bird, two masters of the art of passing, put on a nightly basketball clinic; the give-and-go was never worked to such perfection.

15 GREAT PICKUPS

Don Nelson.

THERE HAVE BEEN TWO CLASSIC types of pickups not acquired through trades. The first has been the older player nearing the end of his career, who still has a little something left and can contribute in a limited capacity. This type truly was a Celtics specialty. Red Auerbach had a genius for handling such players — though, in truth, the opportunity to play for a winner was a key motivation for some. Bill Walton was a perfect example. The second type has been the overlooked gem, a player whose style or attributes make him a successful Celtic even if he has been a failure as a Zephyr or a Laker. Don Nelson was that prototype.

Clyde Lovelette

"Wide Clyde," as he was dubbed by Johnny Most, extended his successful career for two championship seasons when he joined Boston in 1962. The 1952 Olympian and future Hall-of-Famer used a one-hand set shot, in those days an unusual weapon for a 6'-9" widebody, and averaged seven points a game during two years of relief work.

Andy Phillip

Andy Phillip (not pictured) was 34 and ready to hang it up when he answered Auerbach's call and joined the Celtics for the 1956-57 season. Auerbach thought the five-time All-Star and two-time league assist leader would be a perfect backup for Bob Cousy. Phillip gave Boston two quality seasons and picked up his only championship ring.

Willie Naulls

Willie Naulls had been a very successful pro on some very poor Knicks teams when the Celtics signed him prior to the 1963-64 season. Naulls became a starter during his second year in Boston. The one-time UCLA standout averaged a solid 10 points a game and shot 80 percent from the line during his three-year stint in Boston, finishing his career with three championship rings.

Don Nelson

Red acquired "Nellie" after he went unclaimed on waivers early in the 1965-66 season. Don stayed in Boston for 11 years and five championships. He distinguished himself with an unerring medium-range jump shot, a clever inside game, and a reputation as a man to go to in the clutch. The Celtics retired his number, 19 — quite a distinction for a player no other team wanted.

Wayne Embry

This burly and cerebral center was ready to enter the business world when Red Auerbach talked him out of retirement and onto the 1966-67 Celtics. "Wayne the Wall" stayed a second year to get himself a championship ring, then played another year with the expansion Milwaukee Bucks before moving into that team's front office. He is now general manager of the Cleveland Cavaliers.

Bill Walton (see Sixth Men)

16 GREAT MATCHUPS

Wilt and Russell
exchange glances
in front of a young
John Havlicek.

A RECURRING BASKETBALL PLEAsure is the game-within-a-game — the fascinating individual matchups that pit superb players against one another. The Celtics have been involved in many such confrontations, including the most celebrated of them all, Russell vs. Chamberlain. Some one-on-one duels involved well-matched players who were equally proficient on either offense or defense. Others featured a defensive specialist against an offensive virtuoso. All have been spellbinding.

Bill Russell vs. Wilt Chamberlain

Beginning on November 7, 1959, and ending on May 5, 1969, these two titans of the pivot squared off 142 times, not counting All-Star or exhibition games. The game of basketball has not seen such a confrontation since.

Wilt Chamberlain was some five inches taller and at least 50 pounds heavier than Bill Russell. Wilt was always going to score more points and grab more rebounds; both men knew that. What concerned Russell was *when* he would get them. The Celtics have often contended that Russell controlled his foe while the game was being decided early, and that the stat-minded Wilt would load up after Russell had relaxed and the game was out of reach.

The men started their professional rivalry as friends. They would often dine together on the eve of games. As the years went on and their reputations grew in different directions — Russell's as the consummate winner and Wilt's as the frustrated loser — they drifted apart. Ultimately, Russell disdained Chamberlain for not being on the floor for the stretch run of Russell's final championship triumph.

Before that last hurrah, the rivalry stirred fans in Boston, Philadelphia, San Francisco and Los Angeles. Each side accused the other stat crew of fudging rebound totals. Did Wilt really

Fully extended, Bill Russell flicks away Wilt Chamberlain's finger roll. Russell made up for being five inches shorter than Chamberlain with longer arms, a 48-inch vertical leap, and extraordinary timing.

grab 55 rebounds in a losing effort in 1960? That's what the book says. The sheer numbers the two men piled up are astonishing. In those 142 games, Wilt averaged an unusual double — 28.7 points and 28.7 rebounds. Russ averaged 14.5 points and 23.7 rebounds. But the bottom line belonged to Russell and Boston; while Wilt played on some truly powerful teams in those years, Boston won 86, or more than 60 percent, of the games.

Bob Cousy vs. Slater Martin

Most of Bob Cousy's contemporaries cringed at the thought of playing The Cooz at his peak, but Slater "Dugie" Martin was a notable exception. The 5'-10" Martin, who came out of the University of Texas in 1949 and played 11 hard-nosed years in the NBA, was certainly Cousy's most dogged and skillful backcourt foe. Dugie was the backcourt anchor of the five-time champion Minneapolis Lakers. After a brief stay in New York, he moved on to St. Louis, where he was responsible for feeding the ball inside to such stalwarts as Bob Pettit and Cliff Hagan. Martin was a determined defensive player who made Cousy work for everything he got, and Cousy calls him the best he ever played against.

John Havlicek vs. Jerry West

Arguably the greatest duel of midsized players ever, the Havlicek-West matchup reached its peak during the Celtics-Lakers playoff meetings of the 1960s. John Havlicek was a swing man, but over the years saw more and more backcourt duty and took on such defensive challenges as the Lakers' spectacular scoring guard, Jerry West.

Havlicek vs. the Lakers' Jerry West was one of the great matchups in Celtics history, pitting two of the league's very best athletes and clutch performers against each other.

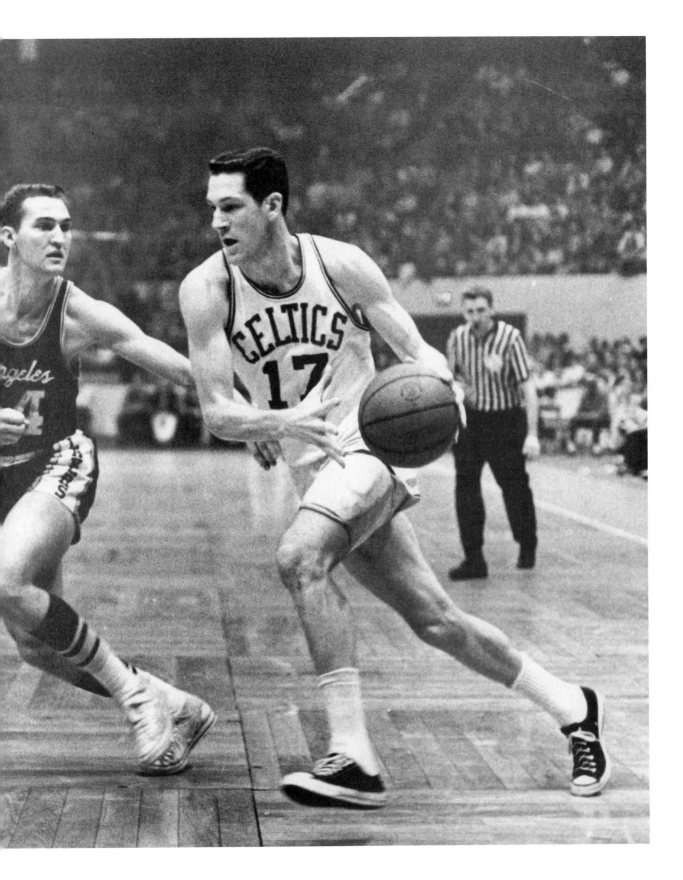

This paired two of the smartest players in the game, as well as two of its most intense competitors. Each was capable of winning games by scoring, rebounding, passing and defending, and each was noted for taking—and usually making—the last shot.

Dave Cowens vs. Kareem Abdul-Jabbar

Dave Cowens had memorable clashes with Willis Reed, Bob Lanier and Bob McAdoo, but the truly epic confrontation for him was his battle with Kareem Abdul-Jabbar. Cowens tried to compensate for Kareem's height advantage with quickness and sheer aggression. Cowens had a two-fold strategy. First, he teased the big man with medium-range jump shots to try and lure him away from the basket. Second, he raced up and down the court in the hopes of beating his rival down the floor for an easy basket and, eventually, wearing him out.

This matchup reached its apex in the 1974 Finals. Kareem single-handedly carried the Bucks to a seventh game, while Cowens tried to stop him with every trick in the book. Kareem won Game Six with a famed sky hook from the right baseline, but two days later Cowens mustered a heroic effort to help Boston wrap up the championship.

For some reason, Kareem seldom acknowledges Cowens as an equal, but the record shows that in one stretch during the 1970s Cowens was on the winning side of the ledger against Kareem in ten consecutive games—a distinction few, if any, of the great center's rivals have shared.

On occasion, Cowens may even have held the taller Abdul-Jabbar.

Paul Silas and Dave DeBusschere, two of the league's fiercest competitors, dueled often during the Celtics-Knicks rivalry in the early 1970s.

Paul Silas vs. Dave DeBusschere

For three seasons, Dave DeBusschere tormented the Celtics. No one could guard the Knicks' star power forward—Satch Sanders was too old, John Havlicek too small, and Steve Kuberski too inexperienced. The solution finally came in the form of a trade for Paul Silas. When Silas stepped on the floor as a Celtic in 1972, Boston finally had its DeBusschere deterrent. He was willing to match the Knick elbow for elbow, shove for shove. Silas could control the boards against DeBusschere and make him sweat on defense. Not that DeBusschere exactly fell apart. He displayed new weapons, taking Silas way outside for jumpers that would be three-pointers today. And he refused to relinquish the inside to this tough new competitor. These were two Ninja warriors, battling hard each time out, their respect for each other growing with every confrontation.

Larry Bird drives past Dr. J.

Larry Bird vs. Julius Erving

The young Larry Bird entered the NBA with one measuring stick for himself: how well he played against the great veteran Julius Erving. "Dr. J" was Bird's very first NBA matchup in an exhibition game his rookie season, and their rivalry evolved into the best one-on-one duel of the time. Erving was quicker, but Bird was stronger. Erving drove better, but Bird shot better. Erving ran the floor, but Bird hit teammates with laser-like passes.

One night in November 1982, the intense emotions overflowed. Bird was on a roll and had scored 42 points early in the third period when suddenly the two superstars squared off. Flashbulbs clicked, but quickly it was over. It was a heat-of-battle thing and didn't affect the respect the two men had for each other as players. When Doc retired, Bird presented him with a piece of the parquet floor — and a little piece of his heart as well.

17 THE VILLAINS

Johnny Most, the Celtics announcer since 1953, sits at his post "high above courtside." Most's colorful announcing has influenced generations of Celtics fans, and his loyalty to the team has caused certain opposing players to bear the wrath of the Garden faithful.

MOST BOSTON OPPONENTS WHO wound up labeled as "villains" were villains primarily to the fans. And they usually got that designation because radio announcer Johnny Most singled them out for playing too dirty (or playing too well).

Wilt Chamberlain

As Bill Russell's chief antagonist, Wilt Chamberlain instantly qualified as villain material. As a frequent complainer that he was being treated too roughly, he further qualified. And as a Goliath in a league of assorted Davids, he qualified again. The truth is that Wilt was essentially mild-mannered both on and off the court, and the league was fortunate that he didn't have much of a temper. But his image in Boston was fixed on one fateful Sunday afternoon, when an altercation broke out and Sam Jones brandished a stool to keep big Wilt at a distance. Chamberlain would never again sell in Boston as a nice guy.

Guy Rodgers

Oh, how Johnny Most loathed Guy Rodgers and his infernal "showboating." It didn't help Rodgers' cause in Boston that he was often compared to Cousy. Johnny waxed euphoric during one playoff game when Rodgers fancy-dribbled himself into a 10-second backcourt violation.

Luke Jackson

Mean and menacing, Luke Jackson was the hulking enforcer for Philadelphia in the 1960s — he stood 6'-9" and weighed 240 pounds. A torn Achilles tendon shortened his career, but not before he helped the Sixers break their Celtics playoff jinx in 1967.

Rudy La Russo

Who could ever forget "Roughhouse Rudy" La Russo? He slugged it out in the trenches with the Celtics' toughest forwards while playing for both the Lakers and the Warriors during the 1960s. For an Ivy League guy (Dartmouth), Rudy sure knew how to throw his elbows.

Luke Jackson.

Rudy LaRusso.

Bailey Howell

Speaking of elbows, another master of that NBA art was Bailey Howell. He must have had radical surgery before joining the Celtics in 1966 because, at least according to Johnny Most, he had always played with at least a dozen elbows with the Bullets and Pistons, but reverted to the more traditional two when he extended his career in green and white.

Oscar Robertson

Oscar Robertson played 14 years in the NBA for Cincinnati and Milwaukee (1960–1974) and never committed a personal foul. At least that's the way he acted every time the refs blew the whistle on him. Johnny Most, for one, didn't like his act at all.

Rick Mahorn, Jeff Ruland, Bill Laimbeer

Johnny Most dubbed them "McFilthy and McNasty", although it was hard to remember which of these Washington Bullets (Mahorn or Ruland) was which. There was a difference between the two. Ruland was an aggressive player who only hurt people by accident. Mahorn was an accident waiting to happen—at all times. Mahorn got to reprise his villain act with a different center when he was traded to the Detroit Pistons, who let him go in the expansion draft in 1989. Bill Laimbeer, with his wandering elbows, is probably far more deserving than Ruland of the "McNasty" label.

Rick Mahorn.

Oscar Robertson.

Rick Barry.

Rick Barry

Rick Barry was another all-time NBA great, in San Francisco, who offended Johnny Most's sense of the game. Most once asked him, "Tell me, Rick, if you had to do it all over again, would you still fall in love with yourself?" True story!

Kareem Abdul-Jabbar

Kareem was too big and too good not to become a villain, a cause he helped along with some visible whining. But Celtics fans treated him with tremendous respect in his final appearances in the Boston Garden.

Dave Zinkoff

He never scored a point, grabbed a rebound, handed out an assist or even coached in the NBA. For 40 years, Dave Zinkoff was the public-address announcer in Philadelphia. Perhaps because his voice was one of the few that could rival Most's for distinctiveness, Johnny always referred to him as "Hysterical Harry" — as in, "Hysterical Harry is at it again!"

Kareem Abdul-Jabbar.

Bill Laimbeer.

ALL-TIME CELTICS ROSTER

(Includes only games played with the Celtics, unless otherwise noted.)

	YEARS	GAMES	MIN.	FIELD GOALS MADE	FIELD GOAL ATTEMPTS	PCT.	FREE THROWS MADE	FREE THROWS ATT.	PCT.
Zaid Abdul-Aziz (Don Smith) 6'-9" Iowa State '68 b. 4/7/46	1 77-78	2	24	3	13	.231	2	3	.667
Mark Acres 6'-11" Oral Roberts '85 b. 11/15/62	2 87-89	141	1783	163	317	.514	97	159	.610
Playoffs	2 88-89	19	160	14	27	.519	9	19	.474
Danny Ainge 6'-5" Brigham Young '81 b. 3/17/59	8 81-89	556	15,603	2537	5210	.487	835	963	.867
Playoffs	8 82-89	112	3354	479	1030	.465	175	211	.829
Jerome Anderson 6'-5" West Virginia '75 b. 10/9/53	1 75-76	22	126	25	45	.556	11	16	.688
Playoffs	1 75-76	4	5	1	3	.333	0	0	.000
Nate Archibald (Tiny) 6'-1" Texas-El Paso '70 b. 9/2/48	5 78-83	363	11,324	1567	3388	.469	1401	1773	.790
Playoffs	4 80-83	41	1400	192	438	.438	160	193	.829
Jim Ard 6'-9" Cincinnati '70 b. 9/19/48	4 74-78	204	2550	292	815	.358	169	243	.695
Playoffs	2 75-76	21	124	14	37	.378	11	14	.786
Dennis Awtrey 6'-10" Santa Clara '70 b. 2/22/48	1 78-79	23	247	17	44	.386	16	20	.800
John Bach 6'-2" Fordham '48 b. 7/10/24	1 48-49	34		34	119	.286	51	75	.680
Tom Barker 6'-11" Hawaii '76 b. 3/11/55	1 78-79	12	131	21	48	.438	11	15	.733
Don Barksdale 6'-6" U.C.L.A. '49 b. 3/31/23	2 53-55	135	3148	423	1114	.380	369	563	.655
Playoffs	2 54-55	13	228	29	76	.382	26	32	813
Jim Barnes (Bad News) 6'-8" Texas Western '64 b. 3/13/41	2 68-70	126	1644	270	636	.425	160	220	.727
Marvin Barnes 6'-9" Providence '74 b. 7/27/52	1 78-79	38	796	133	271	.491	43	66	.652
Jim Barnett 6'-4" Oregon '66 b. 7/7/44	1 66-67	48	383	78	211	.370	42	62	.677
Playoffs	1 66-67	5	26	6	21	.286	2	2	1.000
Ernie Barrett 6'-3" Kansas State '51 b. 7/27/29	2 53-56	131	2092	267	724	.369	107	143	.748
Playoffs	2 54-56	9	106	7	33	.212	5	5	1.000
Moe Becker 6'-1" Duquesne '41 b. 2/24/17	1 46-47	43		70	358	.196	22	44	.500
Hank Beenders 6'-6" Long Island b. 6/2/16	1 48-49	8		6	28	.214	7	9	.778
Bob Bigelow 6'-7" Penn '75 b. 12/26/53	1 77-78	4	17	3	12	.250	0	0	.000
Dave Bing 6'-3" Syracuse '66 b. 10/29/43	1 77-78	80	2256	422	940	.449	244	296	.824
Larry Bird 6'-9" Indiana State '69 b. 12/7/56	10 79-89	717	27,560	7058	14,042	.503	3328	3783	.880
Playoffs	9 80-88	145	6176	1331	2797	.476	825	925	.892
Otis Birdsong Houston '73 b. 12/9/55	1 88-89	13	108	18	36	.500	0	2	.000
Playoffs	1 89	3	20	1	5	.200	0	0	.000
Meyer Bloom (Mike) 6'-6" Temple b. 1/14/15	1 47-48	48		174	640	.272	160	229	.699
Playoffs	1 47-48	3		11	42	262	14	19	.737
Ron Bonham 6'-5" Cincinnati '64 b. 5/31/42	2 64-66	76	681	167	427	.390	144	173	.836
Playoffs	2 65-66	9	29	12	23	.522	7	14	.500
Tom Boswell 6'-9" South Carolina b. 10/2/53	3 75-78	170	2507	401	790	.508	203	282	.720
Playoffs	2 75-77	12	84	9	20	.450	4	6	.667
Harry Boykoff 6'-10" St. John's '47 b. 7/24/22	1 50-51	48		126	336	.375	74	100	.740
Charles Bradley 6'-5" Wyoming '81 b. 5/16/59	2 81-83	102	871	124	298	.416	88	152	.579
Playoffs	2 82-83	9	22	2	8	.250	0	2	.000
Bob Brannum 6'-5" Kentucky, Michigan State b. 5/28/25	4 51-55	279	6576	653	1863	.351	436	689	.633
Playoffs	4 52-55	22	492	53	134	.396	25	47	.532
Carl Braun 6'-5" Colgate '49 b. 9/25/27	1 61-62	48	414	78	207	.377	20	27	.741
Playoffs	1 61-62	6	42	11	28	.393	3	4	.750
Al Brightman 6'-2" Morris Harvey, Southern Cal. b. 1922	1 46-47	58		223	870	.256	121	193	.627
Emmette Bryant 6'-1" DePaul '64 b. 11/4/38	2 68-70	151	3005	407	1008	.404	200	281	.712
Playoffs	1 69	18	607	79	193	.409	40	53	.755
Quinn Buckner 6'-3" Indiana '76 b. 8/20/54	3 82-85	226	3672	460	1077	.427	154	241	.639
Playoffs	3 83-85	45	452	61	138	.442	17	32	.531
Elbert Butler (Al) 6'-2" Niagara '61 b. 7/9/38	1 61-62	59	2008	350	756	.463	131	183	.716
Rick Carlisle 6'-5" Virginia '84 b. 10/27/59	3 84-87	157	1236	148	348	.425	45	60	.750
Playoffs	1 85	10	54	8	15	.533	3	4	.750

On injured list in 84-85 and 86-87.

| REBOUNDS | | | | PERS. FOULS/ | | BLOCKED | | |
OFF.	DEF.	TOT.	ASSISTS	DISQ.	STEALS	SHOTS	PTS.	AVG.
6	9	15	3	4-0	1	1	8	4.0
164	252	416	61	292-2	48	33	424	3.0
14	23	37	2	33-0	1	1	37	1.9
405	1129	1534	2422	1420-17	671	58	6257	11.3
82	200	282	489	340-3	122	11	1211	10.8
4	9	13	6	25-0	3	3	61	2.8
1	0	1	1	1-0	3	3	2	0.5
170	513	683	2563	792-7	326	41	4550	12.5
13	53	66	274	100-1	30	2	546	13.3
233	555	788	142	366-5	43	96	753	3.7
12	16	28	9	34-0	1	4	39	1.9
13	34	47	20	37-0	3	6	50	2.2
			25	24			119	3.5
12	18	30	6	26-0	4	4	53	4.4
		890	246	438-11			1215	9.0
		62	17	40-3			84	6.4
		544	79	336-6			700	5.6
57	120	177	53	144-3	38	39	309	8.1
		53	41	61-0			198	4.1
		4	1	5-0			14	2.8
		343	229	300-6			641	4.9
		13	8	21-0			19	2.1
			30	98			162	3.8
			3	9			19	2.4
1	3	4	0	1-0	0	0	6	1.5
76	136	212	300	247-2	79	18	1088	13.6
1568	5751	7319	4396	1906-9	1300	603	17,899	25.0
343	1204	1547	932	421-1	277	135	3559	24.5
4	9	13	9	10-0	2	1	37	2.8
0	2	2	1	3-0	1	1	2	0.7
			38	116			508	10.6
			2	10			86	12.0
		113	30	62-0			478	6.3
		4	0	3-0			31	3.4
254	411	665	172	511-15	54	23	1005	5.9
10	11	21	7	20-0	1	0	22	1.8
		220	60	197-12			326	6.8
42	74	116	50	145-0	46	33	336	3.3
1	4	5	1	6-0	1	0	4	0.4
		1944	494	1034-42			1742	6.2
		155	36	100-8			131	5.6
		50	71	49-0			176	3.7
		7	2	3-0			25	4.2
			60	115			567	9.8
		461	407	465-14			1014	6.7
		88	54	75-0			198	11.0
129	282	411	637	524-2	255	10	1074	4.8
15	37	52	42	94-1	20	0	139	3.1
		342	203	154-0			831	14.1
38	90	128	164	141-1	30	4	346	2.2
3	2	5	8	9-0	2	0	19	1.9

BOSTON CELTICS YEAR BY YEAR

BOSTON CELTICS WIN-LOSS RECORDS

Year	Home	Road	Neutral	Total
1946-47	14-16	8-22		22-38
1947-48	11-13	9-15		20-28
1948-49	17-12	7-20	1-3	25-35
1949-50	12-14	5-28	5-4	22-46
1950-51	26-6	9-22	4-2	39-30
1951-52	22-7	10-19	7-1	39-27
1952-53	21-3	11-18	14-4	46-25
1953-54	16-6	11-19	15-5	42-30
1954-55	20-5	5-22	11-9	36-36
1955-56	20-7	12-15	7-11	39-33
1956-57	27-4	12-19	5-5	44-28
1957-58	25-4	17-13	7-6	49-23
1958-59	26-4	13-15	13-1	52-20
1959-60	25-2	23-9	11-5	59-16
1960-61	21-7	24-11	12-4	57-22
1961-62	23-5	26-12	11-3	60-20
1962-63	25-5	21-16	12-1	58-22
1963-64	26-4	21-17	12-0	59-21
1964-65	27-3	27-11	8-4	62-18
1965-66	26-5	19-18	9-3	54-26
1966-67	27-4	25-11	8-6	60-21
1967-68	28-9	20-16	6-3	54-28
1968-69	24-12	21-19	3-3	48-34
1969-70	16-21	13-27	5-0	34-48
1970-71	25-14	18-22	1-2	44-38
1971-72	32-9	21-16	3-1	56-26
1972-73	33-6	32-8	3-0	68-14
1973-74	26-6	21-18	9-2	56-26
1974-75	28-13	32-9		60-22
1975-76	31-10	23-18		54-28
1976-77	28-13	16-25		44-38
1977-78	24-17	8-33		32-50
1978-79	21-20	8-33		29-53
1979-80	35-6	26-15		61-21
1980-81	35-6	27-14		62-20
1981-82	35-6	28-13		63-19
1982-83	33-8	23-18		56-26
1983-84	33-8	29-12		62-20
1984-85	35-6	28-13		63-19
1985-86	40-1	27-14		67-15
1986-87	39-2	20-21		59-23
1987-88	36-5	21-20		57-25
1988-89	32-9	10-31		42-40
Totals	1126-343	787-767	202-88	2115-1198

		YEARS	GAMES	MIN.	FIELD GOALS MADE	FIELD GOAL ATTEMPTS	PCT.	FREE THROWS MADE	FREE THROWS ATT.	PCT.
M.L. Carr 6'-6" Guilford '73 b. 1/9/51		6	79-85	363	5810	910	2023	.450	432	570	.758
	Playoffs	6	80-85	64	893	129	341	.378	61	84	.726
Don Chaney 6'-5" Houston '68 b. 3/22/46		10	68-75 77-80	652	14,865	2287	5180	.442	1114	1432	.778
	Playoffs	5	68-69 72-75	59	1423	194	415	.467	94	120	.783
Carlos Clark 6'-4" Mississippi '83 b. 3/10/60		2	83-85	93	689	83	204	.407	57	71	.803
	Playoffs	2	84-85	11	31	7	15	.467	3	4	.750
Ben Clyde 6'-7" Florida State '74 b. 6/10/51		1	74-75	25	157	31	72	.431	7	9	.778
Gene Conley 6'-9" Washington State '52 b. 11/10/30		4	52-53 58-61	235	3696	505	1404	.360	237	362	.655
	Playoffs	3	59-61	33	482	70	187	.374	29	47	.617
Kevin Connors (Chuck) 6'-7" Seton Hall b. 4/10/21		2	47-48	53		99	393	.252	41	87	.471
Norm Cook 6'-9" Kansas '77 b. 3/21/55		1	76-77	25	138	27	72	.375	9	17	.529
	Playoffs	1	77	1	3	2	2	1.000	0	0	.000
Chuck Cooper 6'-5" Duquesne '50 b. 9/29/26		4	50-54	272		639	1873	.341	572	774	.379
	Playoffs	4	51-54	17		39	101	.386	49	62	.790
Mel Counts 7'-0" Oregon State '64 b. 10/16/41		2	64-66	121	1593	321	821	391	178	219	.813
	Playoffs	2	65-66	14	112	18	54	.333	16	18	.889
Bob Cousy 6'-1" Holy Cross '50 b. 9/9/28		13	50-63	917	30,131	6167	16,465	.375	4621	5753	.803
	Playoffs	13	51-63	109	4140	689	2016	.342	640	799	.801
Dave Cowens 6'-8½" Florida State '70 b. 10/25/48		10	70-80	726	28,551	5608	12,193	.460	1975	2527	.782
	Playoffs Also played in 40 games for the Milwaukee Bucks, 1982-83.	7	72-77 80	89	3768	733	1627	.451	218	293	.744
Hal Crisler 6'-3" San Jose State		1	46-47	4		2	6	.333	2	2	1.000
Darren Daye 6'-8" UCLA b. 11/30/60		2	86-88	108	1379	213	419	.508	93	152	.612
	Playoffs	1	87	23	240	42	72	.583	32	37	.865
Dick Dickey 6'-1" North Carolina State '50 b. 10/26/26		1	51-52	45	440	40	136	.294	47	69	.681
	Playoffs	1	52	3	31	1	8	.125	6	7	.857
Ernie Digregorio 6'-0" Providence '73 b. 1/15/51		1	77-78	27	274	47	109	.431	12	13	.923
Bill Dinwiddie 6'-7" New Mexico Highlands '66 b. 7/15/43		2	69-71	61	717	123	328	.375	54	74	.730
Bob Doll 6'-5" Colorado '42 b. 8/10/19		2	48-50	94		265	785	.338	155	231	.671
Bob Donham 6'-2" Ohio State '50 b. 10/11/26		4	50-54	273		662	1379	.480	494	975	.507
	Playoffs	4	51-54	17		31	31	.383	31	76	.408
Steve Downing 6'-8" Indiana '73 b. 9/9/50		2	73-75	27	146	21	66	.318	22	40	.550
	Playoffs	1	74	1	4	1	2	.500	0	0	.000
Terry Duerod 6'-2" Detroit '79 b. 7/29/56		2	80-82	53	260	64	150	.427	17	26	.654
Bob Duffy 6'-4" Tulane b. 7/5/22		1	46-47	17		7	32	.219	5	7	.714
Andy Duncan 6'-6" William & Mary b. 1923		1	50-51	14		7	40	.175	15	22	.682
Ed Ehlers 6'-3" Purdue '47 b. 1924		2	47-49	99		286	1000	.286	228	369	.618
Bob Eliason 6'-2" Hamline '42		1	46-47	1		0	1	.000	0	0	.000
Wayne Embry 6'-8" Miami (Ohio) '58 b. 3/26/37		2	66-68	150	1817	340	842	.404	191	329	.581
	Playoffs	2	67-68	21	200	35	90	.389	15	33	.455
Gene Englund 6'-5" Wisconsin '41 b. 10/21/17 Played in 24 games for Boston and 22 for Tri-Cities in 1949-50.		1	49-50	46		104	274	.380	152	192	.792
John Ezersky 6'-5" St. John's b. 1921 Played 18 games for Boston, 11 for Providence, 27 for Baltimore in 1948-49; played 16 for Boston and 38 for Baltimore in 1949-50.		2	48-50	110		271	894	.303	236	343	.688
Phil Farbman 6'-2" CCNY '48 b. 1924 Played 21 games for Boston, 27 for Philadelphia in 1948-49.		1	48-49	48		60	163	.307	55	81	.679
Bill Fenley 6'-3" Manhattan b. 2/8/22		1	46-47	23		31	138	.225	23	45	.511
Eric Fernsten 6'-10" San Francisco '75 b. 11/1/53		3	79-82	144	912	128	281	.456	72	112	.643
	Playoffs	3	80-82	18	43	3	11	.273	5	8	.625

REBOUNDS			ASSISTS	PERS. FOULS/ DISQ.	STEALS	BLOCKED SHOTS	PTS.	AVG.
OFF.	DEF.	TOT.						
196	532	818	484	675-3	303	95	2285	6.3
50	62	112	58	102-0	35	9	326	5.1
		2572	1268	1840-40	344	160	5689	8.7
			198	108	197-3		482	8.2
36	50	86	65	79-0	43	3	223	2.4
3	0	3	4	5-0	2	2	17	1.5
15	26	41	5	34-1	5	3	69	2.8
			587	110	736-28		1247	5.3
			222	11	119-4		169	5.1
			41	134			239	4.5
10	17	27	5	27-0	10	3	63	2.5
0	0	0	0	0-0	0	0	4	4.0
			1807	494	846-7		1850	6.8
			99	25	73-5		127	7.5
			697	69	341-6		820	6.8
			51	4	36-0		52	3.7
			4781	6945	2231-20		16,955	18.5
			546	937	814-4		2018	18.5
			10,170	2828	2783-86		13,192	18.2
			1285	333	398-15		1684	18.9
				0	6		6	1.5
67	133	200	146	166-0	54	11	519	4.8
11	21	32	13	33-1	9	3	116	5.0
			81	50	79-2		127	2.8
			3	5	7-0		8	2.7
2	25	27	66	22-0	12	1	106	3.9
			209	34	90-1		300	4.9
			225	235			685	7.3
			1071	706	850-31		1818	6.7
			54	38	81-9		93	5.5
14	27	41	11	33-0			64	2.4
			2	0	1-0		2	2.0
8	12	20	18	17-0	8	1	151	2.8
			0	17			19	1.1
			30	8	27-0		29	2.1
			177	211			800	8.1
			0	1			0	0.0
			615	94	311-1		871	5.8
			58	9	45-0		85	4.0
			41	167			360	7.8
			153	237			778	7.0
			36	86			155	3.2
			16	59			85	3.7
81	119	200	46	95-0	28	26	328	2.3
6	5	11	1	4-0	1	3	11	0.6

BOSTON CELTICS COACHING RECORDS

YEAR	COACH	REGULAR SEASON		PLAYOFFS	
		WON	LOST	WON	LOST
1946-47	John (Honey) Russell	22	38	–	–
1947-48	John (Honey) Russell	20	28	1	2
1948-49	Alvin (Doggie) Julian	25	35	–	–
1949-50	Alvin (Doggie) Julian	22	46	–	–
1950-51	Arnold (Red) Auerbach	39	30	0	2
1951-52	Arnold (Red) Auerbach	39	27	1	2
1952-53	Arnold (Red) Auerbach	46	25	3	3
1953-54	Arnold (Red) Auerbach	42	30	2	4
1954-55	Arnold (Red) Auerbach	36	36	3	4
1955-56	Arnold (Red) Auerbach	39	33	1	2
*1956-57	Arnold (Red) Auerbach	44	28	7	3
1957-58	Arnold (Red) Auerbach	49	23	6	5
*1958-59	Arnold (Red) Auerbach	52	20	8	3
*1959-60	Arnold (Red) Auerbach	59	16	8	5
*1960-61	Arnold (Red) Auerbach	57	22	8	2
*1961-62	Arnold (Red) Auerbach	60	20	8	6
*1962-63	Arnold (Red) Auerbach	58	22	8	5
*1963-64	Arnold (Red) Auerbach	59	21	8	2
*1964-65	Arnold (Red) Auerbach	62	18	8	4
*1965-66	Arnold (Red) Auerbach	54	26	11	6
1966-67	Bill Russell	60	21	4	5
*1967-68	Bill Russell	54	28	12	7
*1968-69	Bill Russell	48	34	12	6
1969-70	Tom Heinsohn	34	48	–	–
1970-71	Tom Heinsohn	44	38	–	–
1971-72	Tom Heinsohn	56	26	5	6
1972-73	Tom Heinsohn	68	14	7	6
*1973-74	Tom Heinsohn	56	26	12	6
1974-75	Tom Heinsohn	60	22	6	5
*1975-76	Tom Heinsohn	54	28	12	6
1976-77	Tom Heinsohn	44	38	5	4
1977-78	Tom Heinsohn	11	23		
	Thomas (Satch) Sanders	21	27	–	–
1978-79	Thomas (Satch) Sanders	2	12		
	Dave Cowens	27	41	–	–
1979-80	Bill Fitch	61	21	5	4
*1980-81	Bill Fitch	62	20	12	5
1981-82	Bill Fitch	63	19	7	5
1982-83	Bill Fitch	56	26	2	5
*1983-84	K.C. Jones	62	20	15	8
1984-85	K.C. Jones	63	19	13	8
*1985-86	K.C. Jones	67	15	15	3
1986-87	K.C. Jones	59	23	13	10
1987-88	K.C. Jones	57	25	9	8
1988-89	Jimmy Rodgers	42	40	0	3
TOTALS	Ten Coaches	2115	1198	257	170

* NBA Championships

	YEARS	GAMES	MIN.	FIELD GOALS MADE	FIELD GOAL ATTEMPTS	PCT.	FREE THROWS MADE	FREE THROWS ATT.	PCT.
Henry Finkel (Hank) 7'-0" Dayton '66 b. 4/20/42	6 69-75	436	5277	817	1858	.440	371	572	.649
Playoffs	4 72-75	30	162	27	56	.482	4	6	.667
Jack Foley (The Shot) 6'-3" Holy Cross '62 b. 2/17/40 Played 5 games for Boston, 6 for New York in 1962-63.	1 62-63	11	86	20	52	.385	13	15	.867
Chris Ford 6'-5" Villanova '72 b. 1/11/49	4 78-82	309	9058	1357	2973	.456	354	476	.744
Playoffs	3 80-82	38	924	120	267	.449	32	47	.681
Kevin Gamble 6'-5" Iowa '88 b. 11/13/65	1 88-89	44	375	75	136	.551	35	55	.636
Playoffs	1 89	1	29	4	11	.364	0	2	.000
Jack Garfinkel (Dutch) 6'-0" St. John's b. 6/13/18	3 40-49	92		207	754	.275	62	88	.705
Playoffs	1 48	3		7	23	.304	8	10	.800
Ward Gibson 6'-5" Creighton '47 b. 12/6/21 Played 2 games for Boston, 30 games for Waterloo in 1949-50.	1 49-50	32		67	195	.344	42	64	.656
Artis Gilmore 7'-2" Jacksonville '71 b. 9/21/49	1 87-88	47	521	58	101	.574	48	91	.527
Playoffs	1 87-88	14	86	4	8	.500	7	14	.500
Clarence Glover 6'-8" Western Kentucky '71 b. 11/1/47	1 71-72	25	119	25	55	.455	15	32	.469
Playoffs	1 72	3	10	2	6	.333	2	2	1.000
Mal Graham 6'-1" New York University '67 b. 2/23/45	2 67-69	70	889	130	327	.398	67	102	.657
Playoffs	2 68-69	7	25	2	7	.286	1	3	.333
Ron Grandison 6'-8" New Orleans '87 b. 7/9/64	1 88-89	72	528	59	142	.415	59	80	.738
Playoffs	1 89	0	0	0	0	.000	0	0	.000
Wyndol Gray 6'-1" Harvard, Bowling Green b. 3/20/22	1 46-47	55		139	476	.292	72	124	.581
Sihugo Green 6'-2" Duquesne '56 b. 8/20/34	1 65-66	10	92	12	31	.387	8	16	.500
Gene Guarilia 6'-5" George Washington '59 b. 9/13/27	4 59-63	129	1082	168	447	.376	77	126	.611
Playoffs	2 60-62	12	67	6	26	.231	8	11	.727
Charles Halbert (Chick) 6'-9" West Texas '42 b. 2/27/19	1 48-49	60		202	647	.312	214	345	.620
Cecil Hankins 6'-1" Oklahoma State '46 b. 1/6/22	1 47-48	25		23	116	.198	24	35	.686
Phil Hankinson 6'-8" Penn '73 b. 7/26/51	2 73-75	31	187	56	114	.491	10	13	.769
Playoffs	2 74-75	4	8	3	7	.429	2	2	1.000
Bob Harris (Gabby) 6'-7" Oklahoma State '49 b. 3/16/27	4 50-54	263		636	1626	.391	461	734	.628
Playoffs	4 51-54	17		42	91	.462	44	59	.746
John Havlicek 6'-5" Ohio State '62 b. 4/8/40	16 62-78	1270	46,471	10,513	23,930	.439	5369	6589	.815
Playoffs	13 63-69 72-77	172	6860	1451	3329	.436	874	1046	.836
John Hazen 6'-2" Indiana State b. 1927	1 48-49	6		6	17	.353	6	7	.857
Tom Heinsohn 6'-7" Holy Cross '56 b. 8/26/34	9 56-65	654	19,254	4773	11,787	.405	2648	3353	.790
Playoffs	9 59-65	104	3223	818	2035	.402	422	566	.743
Dixon Hemric (Dick) 6'-6" Wake Forest '55 b. 8/29/33	2 55-57	138	2384	270	717	.377	323	483	.669
Playoffs	2 56-57	5	73	6	31	.194	9	16	.563
Gerald Henderson 6'-2" Virginia Commonwealth '78 b. 1/16/56	5 79-84	400	8152	1467	3002	.489	559	768	.728
Playoffs	5 80-84	67	1442	244	538	.454	106	149	.711
Conner Henry 6'-7" Calif-Santa Barbara '86 b. 7/21/63	2 86-88	46	312	49	131	.374	19	27	.704
Playoffs	1 87	11	35	8	16	.500	5	10	.500
Clarence Hermsen (Kleggie) 6'-9" Minnesota '48 b. 3/12/23	1 50-51	71		189	644	.293	155	237	.654
Playoffs	1 51	2		1	6	.167	0	0	.000
Sidney Hertzberg (Sonny) 6'-0" CCNY b. 7/29/22	2 49-50	133		481	1516	.317	366	461	.794
Playoffs	1 51	2		3	13	.231	4	5	.800
Jack Hewson 6'-6" Temple '48 b. 9/7/24	1 47-48	24		22	89	.247	21	30	.700
Mel Hirsch 5'-6" Brooklyn '43 b. 7/31/21	1 46-47	13		9	45	.200	1	2	.500
Chuck Hoefer 5'-9" Hofstra b. 7/12/22 Played 35 games for Boston, 23 for Toronto in 1946-47.	2 46-48	65		133	533	.250	95	147	.646
Bob Houbregs 6'-8" Washington '53 b. 3/12/32 Played 2 games for Boston, 62 for Baltimore and Ft. Wayne in 1954-55.	1 54-55	64	1326	148	386	.383	129	182	.709

REBOUNDS OFF.	DEF.	TOT.	ASSISTS	PERS. FOULS/DISQ.	STEALS	BLOCKED SHOTS	PTS.	AVG.
		1605	328	823-23			2005	4.6
		46	13	26-0			58	1.9
		16	5	8-0			53	4.8
316	392	708	1021	733-4	367	84	3194	10.3
28	57	85	82	97-1	30	8	283	7.4
11	31	42	34	40-0	14	3	187	4.3
1	0	1	2	1-0	1		8	8.0
			134	159			476	5.2
			7	15			22	7.3
			37	106			176	5.5
54	94	148	12	94-0	10	18	164	3.5
4	16	20	1	14-0	0	4	15	1.1
		46	4	26-0			65	2.6
		3	0	1-0			6	2.0
		118	75	150-0			327	4.7
		4	2	3-0			5	0.7
47	45	92	42	71-0	18	3	177	2.5
0	0	0	0	0-0	0	0	0	0.0
		47		105			350	6.4
		11	9	16-0			32	3.2
		294	36	146-1			413	3.2
		23	4	10-0			20	1.7
		113		175			618	10.3
		8		28			70	2.8
23	34	57	6	21-0	4	1	122	3.9
2	1	3	0	0-0	0	2	8	2.0
		1824	373	813-23			1733	6.6
		120	21	73-5			128	7.5
		8007	6114	3281-21			26,395	20.8
		1186	825	517-9			3776	22.0
			3	10			18	3.0
		6749	1318	2454-58			12194	18.6
		954	215	417-14			2058	19.8
		703	102	240-2			863	6.3
		31	2	8-0			21	4.2
252	386	638	1107	871-10	418	65	3521	8.8
57	69	126	214	165-1	73	7	597	8.9
9	28	37	39	38-0	7	2	132	2.9
3	3	6	0	3-0	0	0	22	2.0
		448	92	261-8			533	7.5
		3	0	6-0			2	1.0
		260	444	309			1328	10.0
		2	3	8			10	5.0
			1	39			65	2.7
			10	18			19	1.5
			36	159			361	5.6
		297	86	180-5			425	6.6

BOSTON CELTICS COACHING RECORDS

COACH	REGULAR SEASON RECORD (BOSTON ONLY)		PLAYOFF RECORD	
John Russell	42-66	(.389)	1-2	(.333)
Alvin Julian	47-81	(.367)	0-0	(.000)
Red Auerbach	795-397	(.667)	90-58	(.608)
Bill Russell	167-83	(.661)	28-18	(.609)
Tom Heinsohn	427-263	(.619)	47-33	(.588)
Tom Sanders	23-39	(.371)	0-0	(.000)
Dave Cowens	27-41	(.397)	0-0	(.000)
Bill Fitch	242-86	(.738)	26-19	(.578)
K.C. Jones	308-102	(.751)	65-37	(.637)
Jimmy Rodgers	42-40	(.512)	0-3	(.000)
TOTALS	2115-1198	(.638)	257-170	(.602)

CELTICS CAREER LEADERS Regular Season
(through 1988–89)

GAMES

1. John Havlicek 1,270
2. Bill Russell 983
3. Bob Cousy 917
4. Tom Sanders 916
5. Don Nelson 872
6. Sam Jones 871
7. Dave Cowens 726
8. Jo Jo White 717
9. Larry Bird 717
10. Robert Parish 714

MINUTES

1. John Havlicek 46,471
2. Bill Russell 40,726
3. Bob Cousy 30,131
4. Dave Cowens 28,551
5. Larry Bird 27,550
6. Jo Jo White 26,770
7. Sam Jones 24,285
8. Robert Parish 23,722
9. Kevin McHale 22,275
10. Tom Sanders 22,164

POINTS

1. John Havlicek 26,335
2. Larry Bird 17,999
3. Bob Cousy 16,955
4. Sam Jones 15,411
5. Bill Russell 14,522
6. Dave Cowens 13,192
7. Jo Jo White 13,188
8. Kevin McHale 12,830
9. Robert Parish 12,820
10. Bill Sharman 12,287

AVERAGE POINTS (3 Yrs. Min.)

1. Larry Bird 25.0
2. John Havlicek 20.8
3. Ed Macauley 18.9
4. Tom Heinsohn 18.6
5. Bob Cousy 18.5
6. Kevin McHale 18.5
7. Jo Jo White 18.3

		YEARS	GAMES	MIN.	FIELD GOALS MADE	FIELD GOAL ATTEMPTS	PCT.	FREE THROWS MADE	FREE THROWS ATT.	PCT.
Bailey Howell 6'-7" Mississippi State '59 b. 1/20/37		4	66-70	323	9909	2290	4766	.480	1232	1666	.739
	Playoffs	3	67-69	46	1389	306	615	.498	140	201	.697
Tracy Jackson 6'-6" Notre Dame '81 b. 4/21/59		1	81-82	11	66	10	26	.385	6	10	.600
John Janisch 6'-3" Valparaiso '46 b. 3/15/20 Played 3 games for Boston, 7 for Providence in 1947-48.		1	47-48	10		14	50	.280	9	16	.563
Dennis Johnson 6'-4" Pepperdine '76 b. 9/18/54		6	83-89	466	16,285	2411	5398	.447	1409	1677	.840
	Playoffs	6	84-89	104	4096	643	1469	.438	429	513	.836
Rich Johnson 6'-9" Grambling '68 b. 12/18/46		3	68-71	97	1074	200	442	.452	57	93	.613
	Playoffs	1	69	2	4	1	1	1.000	0	0	.000
Johnny Jones 6'-7" Los Angeles State '67 b. 3/12/43		1	67-68	51	475	46	253	.340	42	68	.454
	Playoffs	1	68	5	10		6	.500	0	0	.000
K.C. Jones 6'-1" San Francisco '56 b. 5/25/32		9	58-67	675	17,472	1914	4944	.387	1171	1853	.612
	Playoffs	9	59-67	105	2494	241	656	.367	186	269	.691
Sam Jones 6'-4" North Carolina Central '57 b. 6/24/33		12	57-69	871	24,285	6271	13,745	.456	2869	3572	.803
	Playoffs	12	58-69	154	4654	1149	2571	.447	611	753	.811
Jeff Judkins 6'-6" Utah '78 b. 3/23/56		2	78-80	146	2195	434	863	.503	181	222	.816
	Playoffs	1	80	7	10	4	8	.500	0	0	.000
George Kaftan 6'-3" Holy Cross '59 b. 2/22/28 Also played 136 games for New York Knicks and Baltimore, 1950-51 through 1952-53.		2	48-50	76		315	850	.371	208	323	.644
Tony Kappen 5'-10" b. 4/13/19 Played 18 games for Boston, 41 for Pittsburgh in 1946-47.		1	46-47	59		128	537	.238	128	161	.795
Gerard Kelly (Jerry) 6'-2" Marshall b. 1922		1	46-47	43		91	313	.291	74	111	.667
Tom Kelly 6'-2" New York University '48 b. 3/5/24		1	48-49	27		73	218	.335	45	73	.616
Thomas Kimball (Toby) 6'-8" Connecticut '65 b. 9/23/42		1	66-67	38	222	35	97	.361	27	40	.675
	Playoffs	1	67	1	4	3	2	.000	0	0.000	
Maurice King 6'-3" Kansas '57 b. 3/12/35		1	59-60	1	19	5	8	.625	0	1	.000
Bob Kinney 6'-6" Rice '42 b. 9/16/20 Played 21 games for Boston, 37 games for Fort Wayne in 1948-49.		2	48-49	118		394	1116	.353	337	554	.608
Greg Kite 6'-11" Brigham Young '83 b. 8/5/61		5	83-88	241	1916	153	378	.405	72	169	.426
	Playoffs	4	84-87	53	351	20	50	.400	13	22	.591
Joe Kleine 7'-0" Arkansas '84 b. 1/4/62		1	88-89	28	498	59	129	.457	53	64	.828
	Playoffs	1	89	3	65	6	11	.545	7	9	.778
Billy Knight 6'-6" Pittsburgh '74 b. 6/9/52		1	78-79	40	1119	219	436	.502	118	146	.808
Harold Kottman 6'-8" Culver-Stockton '46 b. 8/22/22		1	46-47	53		59	188	.314	47	101	.465
Wayne Kreklow 6'-4" Drake '79 b. 1/4/57		1	80-81	25	100	11	47	.234	7	10	.700
Steve Kuberski 6'-8" Bradley '69 b. 11/6/47		8	69-74 75-78	499	7285	1185	2829	.419	559	731	.765
	Playoffs	4	72-74 76	50	614	110	239	.460	65	84	.774
Frank Kudelka (Apples) 6'-2" St. Mary's (Calif.) b. 1925		1	50-51	62		179	518	.346	83	119	.697
	Playoffs	1	50-51	1		2	4	.500	0	3	.000
Tony Lavelli 6'-3" Yale '49 b. 7/11/26		1	49-50	56		162	436	.372	168	197	.853
Ed Leede 6'-3" Dartmouth '48 b. 7/17/27		2	49-51	121		293	877	.335	363	505	.719
	Playoffs	1	51	2		1	7	.143	1	1	1.000
Reggie Lewis 6'-7" Northeastern '87 b. 11/21/65		2	87-89	130	3062	694	1435	.484	324	418	.775
	Playoffs	2	88-89	15	195	39	89	.438	12	18	.667
Brad Lohaus 7'-0" Iowa '87 b. 9/29/64		2	87-89	118	1456	239	516	.463	85	108	.787
	Playoffs	1	88	9	26	8	11	.727	0	0	.000
Jim Loscutoff 6'-5" Oregon '55 b. 2/4/30		9	55-64	511	9431	1333	3868	.345	490	750	.653
	Playoffs	7	56-57 59-64	58	997	136	420	.324	48	79	.608
Clyde Lovelette 6'-9" Kansas '52 b. 9/7/29		2	62-64	106	1005	289	681	.424	118	155	.761
	Playoffs	2	63-64	11	80	15	60	.250	8	10	.800

REBOUNDS OFF.	DEF.	TOT.	ASSISTS	PERS. FOULS/ DISQ.	STEALS	BLOCKED SHOTS	PTS.	AVG.
		2717	493	1127-15			5812	18.0
		330	46	203-11			752	16.3
7	5	12	5	5-0	3	0	26	2.4
			2	5			37	3.7
385	1171	1556	3001	1297-14	573	219	6274	13.5
118	293	411	710	329-3	138	37	1733	16.7
		265	39	198-3			457	4.7
		2	0	0-0			2	1.0
		114	26	60-0			214	4.2
		4	0	2-0			6	1.2
		2392	2904	1824-25			4999	7.4
		320	396	335-4			668	6.4
		4305	2209	1735-5			15,411	17.7
		718	358	391-5			2909	18.9
102	155	257	192	275-1	110	17	1060	7.3
3	1	4	0	0-0	1	0	9	1.3
			206	120			838	11.0
			28	78			384	6.5
			21	128			256	6.0
			38	73			191	7.1
		146	13	42-0			97	2.6
		3	0	1-0			0	0.0
		4	2	3-0			10	10.0
			177	475			1125	9.5
171	301	472	70	371-6	27	97	378	1.6
30	60	90	17	85-1	5	13	53	1.0
49	88	137	32	66-0	15	5	171	6.1
4	13	17	2	9-0	0	1	19	6.3
41	132	173	66	86-1	31	3	556	13.9
			17	58			165	3.1
2	10	12	9	20-0	2	1	30	1.2
		1998	300	846-3			2929	5.9
		148	24	85-0			285	5.7
		158	105	211-8			441	7.1
		5	2	3-0			4	4.0
			40	107			492	8.8
		118	225	311			949	7.8
		0	2	3			3	1.5
144	296	440	244	312-5	140	87	1715	13.2
14	23	37	15	24-0	8	2	90	6.0
93	187	280	98	224-2	41	67	566	4.8
1	3	4	0	4-0	0	1	16	1.8
		2808	353	1497-40			3156	6.2
		299	32	219-8			320	5.5
		303	51	237-0			696	6.6
		12	3	21-0			38	3.5

CELTICS CAREER LEADERS
(continued)

8.   Dave Cowens 18.2
9.   Bill Sharman 18.1
10. Bailey Howell 18.0

FIELD GOALS ATTEMPTED

1.   John Havlicek 23,930
2.   Bob Cousy 16,465
3.   Larry Bird 14,042
4.   Sam Jones 13,745
5.   Bill Russell 12,930
6.   Jo Jo White 12,782
7.   Dave Cowens 12,193
8.   Tom Heinsohn 11,787
9.   Bill Sharman 10,807
10. Robert Parish 9,500

FIELD GOALS MADE

1.   John Havlicek 10,513
2.   Larry Bird 7,058
3.   Sam Jones 6,271
4.   Bob Cousy 6,167
5.   Bill Russell 5,687
6.   Jo Jo White 5,648
7.   Dave Cowens 5,608
8.   Robert Parish 5,253
9.   Kevin McHale 5,057
10. Tom Heinsohn 4,773

FIELD GOAL PERCENTAGE
(2.000 Attempts)

1.   Kevin McHale 585 (5,057-8,858)
2.   Cedric Maxwell 559 (7,285-4,984)
3.   Robert Parish 553 (5,253-9,500)
4.   Rick Robey 510 (1,144-2,241)
5.   Larry Bird 503 (7,086-14,042)
6.   Gerald Henderson 480 (1,467-3,002)
7.   Danny Ainge 487 (2,537-5,218)
8.   Don Nelson .484 (3,717-7,672)
9.   Bailey Howell 480 (2,230-4,766)
10. Nate Archibald 469 (1,567-3,338)

FREE THROWS ATTEMPTED

1.   John Havlicek 6,589
2.   Bob Cousy 5,763
3.   Bill Russell 5,614
4.   Larry Bird 3,783
5.   Sam Jones 3,572
6.   Ed Macauley 3,518
7.   Cedric Maxwell 3,496
8.   Kevin McHale 3,481
9.   Bill Sharman 3,451
10. Tom Heinsohn 3,353

FREE THROWS MADE

1.   John Havlicek 5,369
2.   Bob Cousy 4,521
3.   Larry Bird 3,325
4.   Bill Russell 3,148
5.   Bill Sharman 3,047
6.   Sam Jones 2,369
7.   Cedric Maxwell 2,738
8.   Ed Macauley 2,724
9.   Kevin McHale 2,715
10. Tom Heinsohn 2,648

		YEARS	GAMES	MIN.	FIELD GOALS MADE	FIELD GOAL ATTEMPTS	PCT.	FREE THROWS MADE	FREE THROWS ATT.	PCT.
Al Lucas 6'-3" Fordham b. 7/4/22	1	48-49	2		1	3	.333	0	0	.000
Ed Macauley (Easy Ed) 6'-8" St. Louis '49 b. 3/22/28	6	50-56	416		2579	5796	.447	2724	3518	.774
Playoffs	6	51-56	26		138	301	.458	122	167	.731
John Mahnken 6'-8" Georgetown '45 b. 6/16/22	4	49-53	249		297	1325	.224	187	284	.658
Playoffs (Played in 24 games for Boston, 2 games for Ft. Wayne and 36 games for Tri-Cities in 1949-50. Played for both Boston and Indianapolis in 1950-51.)	2	52-53	9	122	2	17	.118	8	11	.727
Francis Mahoney (Mo) 6'-4" Brown '50 b. 11/20/27	1	52-53	6	34	4	10	.400	4	5	.800
Playoffs	1	53	4	45	3	14	.214	3	5	.600
Pete Maravich 6'-5" Louisiana State '70 b. 6/22/48	1	79-80	26	442	123	249	.494	50	55	.909
Playoffs	1	80	9	104	25	51	.490	2	3	.667
Saul Mariaschin 5'-11" Harvard '47 b. 8/10/24	1	47-48	43		125	463	.270	83	117	.709
Playoffs	1	48	2		10	42	.238	9	14	.643
Cedric Maxwell 6'-8" U.N.C. Charlotte '77 b. 11/21/55	8	77-85	607	18,495	2786	4984	.559	2738	3496	.783
Playoffs Three-point goals: 1983-84, 0-for-1 (.000). (Played in 228 regular season games for L.A. Clippers and Houston, 1985-86 through 1987-88.)	6	80-85	88	2539	356	652	.546	340	436	.780
Bob McAdoo 6'-9" North Carolina '73 b. 9/25/51 (Played 40 games for New York Knicks in 1978-79.)	1	78-79	20	637	167	334	.500	77	115	.670
John McCarthy 6'-1" Canisius '56 b. 4/25/34	1	63-64	28	206	16	48	.333	5	13	.385
Playoffs	1	64	1	8	1	1	1.000	0	0	.000
Glenn McDonald 6'-6" Long Beach State '74 b. 3/18/52	2	74-76	137	1414	261	638	.409	68	93	.731
Playoffs	2	75-76	19	98	10	38	.263	6	9	.667
Kevin McHale 6'-10" Minnesota '89 b. 12/19/57	9	80-89	694	22,275	5057	8958	.565	2715	3481	.780
Playoffs	9	81-89	139	4729	987	1747	.565	628	805	.780
Horace McKinney (Bones) 6'-6" North Carolina '46 b. 1/1/19	2	50-51	107		238	745	.319	123	161	.764
Playoffs	2	51-52	5		13	34	.382	4	5	.800
Dick Mehen 6'-6" Tennessee '47 b. 5/20/22	1	50-51	66		192	532	.361	90	123	.732
Ed Mikan 6'-8" DePaul '48 b. 10/20/25	1	53-54	9	71	8	24	.333	5	9	.556
Dirk Minniefield 6'-3" Kentucky '83 b. 1/17/61	1	87-88	61	868	83	173	.480	27	32	.844
Playoffs	1	88	11	50	6	14	.429	2	2	1.000
Mark Minor 6'-5" Ohio State '72 b. 5/14/50	1	72-73	4	20	1	4	.250	3	4	.750
Rex Morgan 6'-5" Jacksonville '70 b. 10/27/48	2	70-72	62	416	57	152	.375	58	85	.682
Playoffs	1	72	4	10	1	7	.143	1	3	.333
Dwight Morrison (Red) 6'-8" Idaho '54 b. 1931	2	54-56	142	2137	209	524	.399	116	204	.569
Playoffs	2	55-56	10	65	5	15	.333	1	7	.143
Joe Mullaney 6'-0" Holy Cross '59 b. 11/17/25	1	49-50	37		9	70	.129	12	15	.800
George Munroe 5'-11" Dartmouth '43 b. 1/5/22	1	47-48	21		27	91	.297	17	26	.654
Playoffs	1	48	3		1	5	.200	2	2	1.000
Dick Murphy 6'-1" Manhattan b. 1921 (Played 7 games for Boston, 24 for New York in 1946-47.)	1	46-47	31		15	75	.200	4	9	.444
Willie Naulls 6'-6" U.C.L.A. '56 b. 10/7/34	3	63-66	220	4307	951	2370	.401	372	464	.802
Playoffs	3	64-66	33	432	85	225	.378	44	59	.746
Don Nelson 6'-6" Iowa '62 b. 5/15/40	11	65-76	872	18,970	3717	7672	.484	2534	3296	.769
Playoffs	9	66-69 72-76	134	2941	554	1109	.500	385	470	.819
Jack Nichols 6'-7" Washington '48 b. 4/9/26	5	53-58	329	8077	1107	3004	.369	618	798	.774
Playoffs	5	54-58	37	807	120	302	.397	62	79	.785
Rich Niemann 7'-0" St. Louis '68 b. 7/2/46	1	69-70	6	18	2	5	.400	2	2	1.000
Bob Nordmann 6'-10" St. Louis '61 b. 12/11/39	1	64-65	3	25	3	5	.600	0	0	.000
George Nostrand 6'-8" Wyoming '46 b. 4/5/24 (Played 27 games for Boston and 33 games for Providence in 1948-49. Played 18 games for Boston, 36 games for Chicago and 1 for Tri-Cities in 1949-50.)	2	48-50	115		290	906	.320	221	383	.577

| REBOUNDS | | | | PERS. | | BLOCKED | | |
OFF.	DEF.	TOT.	ASSISTS	FOULS/DISQ.	STEALS	SHOTS	PTS.	AVG.
				2	0		2	1.0
		3367	1521	1064-7			7882	18.9
		197	98	79-3			398	15.0
		533	323	595-9			981	3.9
		29	9	27-1			12	1.3
			7	1	7-0		12	2.0
			7	2	14-0		9	2.3
10	28	38	29	49-1	9	2	299	11.5
0	8	8	6	12-0	3	0	54	6.0
				60	121		333	7.7
				1	12		29	9.7
1618	2405	4023	1390	1768-32	549	378	8311	13.7
221	298	519	176	242-1	70	50	1052	11.9
36	105	141	40	55-1	12	20	411	20.6
		35	24	42-0			37	1.3
		1	1	0-0			2	2.0
76	127	203	92	181-0	47	25	590	4.3
2	12	14	6	16-0	2	0	26	1.4
1798	3479	5277	1217	2076-21	262	1269	12,830	18.5
400	646	1046	225	472-8	51	245	2603	18.7
		373	196	284-10			599	5.6
		16	10	18-0			30	6.0
		223	188	149-4			474	7.2
		20	3	15-0			21	2.3
22	53	75	190	107-0	44	3	196	3.2
1	1	2	11	13-0	2	0	16	1.5
			4	2	5-0		5	1.3
			91	39	92-2		172	2.8
			6	0	6-0		3	0.8
			796	135	381-15		534	3.8
			25	1	27-1		14	1.1
				52	30		30	0.8
				3	20		71	3.4
				1	2		4	1.3
				8	15		34	1.1
			1011	208	630-9		2274	10.3
			113	18	81-1		217	6.6
			4517	1354	2094-16		9968	11.4
			647	189	357-4		1493	11.1
			2197	556	961-24		2932	8.6
			209	79	109-2		302	8.2
			6	2	10-0		6	1.0
			8	3	5		6	2.0
				123	282-0		801	7.0

CELTICS CAREER LEADERS
(continued)

FREE THROW PERCENTAGE
(1.300 Attempts)

1. Bill Sharman .... .883 (3,047-3,451)
2. Larry Bird .... .880 (3,328-3,783)
3. Larry Siegfried .... .855 (1,500-1,755)
4. Dennis Johnson .... .840 (1,409-1,577)
5. Jo Jo White .... .833 (1,892-2,270)
6. John Havlicek .... .815 (5,369-6,589)
7. Frank Ramsey .... .804 (2,480-3,083)
8. Bob Cousy .... .803 (4,621-6,753)
9. Sam Jones .... .803 (2,869-3,572)
10. Nate Archibald .... .790 (1,401-1,773)

ASSISTS

1. Bob Cousy 6,945
2. John Havlicek 6,114
3. Larry Bird 4,396
4. Bill Russell 4,100
5. Jo Jo White 3,686
6. Dennis Johnson 3,001
7. K.C. Jones 2,804
8. Dave Cowens 2,628
9. Nate Archibald 2,563
10. Danny Ainge 2,422

REBOUNDS

1. Bill Russell 21,820
2. Dave Cowens 10,170
3. John Havlicek 8,007
4. Robert Parish 7,412
5. Larry Bird 7,319
6. Tom Sanders 5,798
7. Tom Heinsohn 5,749
8. Kevin McHale 5,277
9. Bob Cousy 4,731
10. Don Nelson 4,517

PERSONAL FOULS

1. John Havlicek 3,281
2. Tom Sanders 3,044
3. Dave Cowens 2,783
4. Bill Russell 2,592
5. Tom Heinsohn 2,454
6. Bob Cousy 2,231
7. Robert Parish 2,176
8. Frank Ramsey 2,158
9. Don Nelson 2,094
10. Kevin McHale 2,076

DISQUALIFICATIONS

1. Tom Sanders 94
2. Frank Ramsey 87
3. Dave Cowens 86
4. Tom Heinsohn 58
5. Bob Brannum 42
6. Robert Parish 42
7. Don Chaney 40
8. Jim Loscutoff 40
9. Cedric Maxwell 32
10. Bob Donham 31

	YEARS	GAMES	MIN.	FIELD GOALS MADE	FIELD GOAL ATTEMPTS	PCT.	FREE THROWS MADE	FREE THROWS ATT.	PCT.
Stan Noszka 6'-1" Duquesne '43 b. 9/19/20	2 47-49	52		57	220	.259	39	65	.600
Playoffs	1 48	3		10	30	.333	5	8	.625
Dermott O'Connell (Dermie) 6'-0" Holy Cross '49 b. 4/13/28 (Played 37 games for Boston and 24 games for St. Louis in 1949-50.)	2 48-50	82		198	740	.268	77	145	.531
Enoch Olsen (Bud) 6'-8" Louisville '62 b. 7/25/40	1 68-69	7	43	7	19	.368	0	6	.000
Togo Palazzi 6'-4" Holy Cross '54 b. 8/8/32	3 54-57	179	2220	456	1197	.381	266	359	.741
Playoffs (Played in 20 games for Boston and 43 for Syracuse in 1956-57.)	2 55-56	7	37	13	29	.448	5	10	.500
Robert Parish 7'-½" Centenary '76 b. 8/30/53	9 80-89	714	23,722	5253	9500	.553	2314	3195	.724
Playoffs	9 81-89	139	4902	903	1804	.500	452	625	.723
Jim Paxson 6'-6" Dayton '79 b. 7/9/57	2 87-89	102	1939	339	743	.456	152	182	.835
Playoffs	1 88	15	188	17	59	.288	16	20	.800
Andy Phillip 6'-2" Illinois '47 b. 3/7/22	2 56-58	137	2640	202	550	.367	130	208	.625
Playoffs	2 57-58	20	219	13	43	.302	13	24	.542
Gary Phillips 6'-3" Houston '61 b. 7/7/39	1 61-62	72	693	110	320	.344	50	86	.581
Playoffs	1 62	6	32	1	16	.062	8	11	.727
Ed Pinckney 6'-9" Villanova '84 b. 3/27/63	1 88-89	29	678	95	196	.540	103	129	.798
Playoffs	1 89	3	45	3	12	.250	2	2	1.000
Frank Ramsey 6'-3" Kentucky '53 b. 7/13/31	9 54-55 56-64	623	15,330	2949	7382	.399	2480	3083	.804
Playoffs	9 55 57-64	98	2396	469	1105	.424	393	476	.826
John Richter 6'-9" North Carolina State b. 3/12/37	1 59-60	66	808	113	332	.340	59	117	.504
Playoffs	1 60	8	95	15	38	.395	5	14	.357
Mel Riebe 5'-11" Ohio University b. 7/12/16	2 47-49	91		374	1242	.301	164	270	.607
Playoffs (Played 33 games for Boston, 10 for Providence in 1948-49.)	1 48	3		14	43	.326	14	20	.700
Arnie Risen 6'-9" Ohio State b. 10/9/24	3 55-58	174	3651	442	1197	.369	390	563	.693
Playoffs	3 56-58	33	408	52	149	.349	54	80	.675
Ramon Rivas 6'-10" Temple '88 b. 6/3/66	1 88-89	28	91	12	31	.387	16	25	.640
Bill Roberts 6'-9" Wyoming b. 1925 (Played 26 games for Boston, 22 for St. Louis, 2 for Chicago in 1948-49.)	1 48-49	50		89	267	.333	44	63	.698
Fred Roberts 6'-10" Brigham Young '82 b. 8/14/60	2 86-88	147	2111	300	600	.500	252	318	.792
Playoffs	2 87-88	35	365	41	80	.513	38	55	.691
Rick Robey 6'-10" Kentucky '78 b. 1/30/56	5 78-83	339	6442	1144	2241	.510	541	858	.631
Playoffs	4 80-83	43	567	80	178	.449	38	70	.543
Ken Rollins 6'-0" Kentucky '48 b. 9/14/23	1 52-53	43	426	38	115	.330	22	27	.815
Playoffs	1 53	6	65	6	15	.400	8	8	1.000
Curtis Rowe 6'-7" U.C.L.A. '71 b. 7/2/49	3 76-79	183	4323	589	1251	.471	288	404	.714
Playoffs	1 77	9	237	32	68	.471	22	29	.759
Bill Russell 6'-10" San Francisco '56 b. 2/12/34	13 56-69	963	40,726	5687	12,930	.440	3148	5614	.561
Playoffs	13 57-69	165	7497	1003	2335	.430	667	1106	.603
Ed Sadowski 6'-5" Seton Hall b. 7/11/17	1 47-48	47		308	953	.323	294	422	.697
Playoffs	1 48	3		19	55	.345	23	38	.605
Kenny Sailors 5'-10" Wyoming '46 b. 1/14/22	1 50-51	60		181	533	.340	131	180	.728
Frankie Sanders 6'-6" Southern '78 b. 1/23/57	1 78-79	24	216	55	119	.462	22	27	.815
Tom Sanders (Satch) 6'-6" New York University '60 b. 11/8/38	13 60-73	916	22,164	3416	7988	.428	1934	2520	.767
Playoffs	11 61-69 72-73	130	3039	465	1066	.436	212	296	.716
Woodrow Sauldsberry (Woody) 6'-7" Texas Southern '57 b. 7/11/34	1 65-66	39	530	80	249	.321	11	22	.500
Fred Saunders 6'-7" Syracuse '74 b. 7/13/51	2 76-78	94	1294	214	486	.440	49	70	.700
Playoffs	1 77	9	66	12	33	.364	5	6	.833

| REBOUNDS | | | ASSISTS | PERS. FOULS/DISQ. | STEALS | BLOCKED SHOTS | PTS. | AVG. |
OFF.	DEF.	TOT.						
			29	108			153	2.9
			2	11			25	8.3
			156	131			473	5.8
		14	4	6-0			14	2.0
		590	121	264-2			1178	6.6
		16	1	8-0			31	4.4
2314	5098	7412	1298	2176-42	894	1231	12,820	18.0
415	957	1372	184	480-14	124	257	2258	16.2
33	86	119	183	169-0	68	13	866	8.5
1	8	9	11	18-0	6	2	50	3.3
		339	289	242-1			534	3.9
		34	24	38-0			39	2.0
		107	63	109-0			270	3.7
		3	1	6-0			10	1.7
60	88	148	44	77-1	29	23	293	10.1
2	3	5	1	7-0	1	1	8	2.7
		3410	1134	2158-87			8378	13.4
		494	151	362-14			1331	13.6
		312	27	158-1			285	4.3
		29	2	17-1			35	4.4
			145	247			912	10.0
			3	10			42	14.0
		1199	191	658-26			1274	7.3
		164	19	95-6			158	6.9
9	15	24	3	21-0	4	1	40	1.4
			41	113			222	4.4
114	238	352	143	247-1	38	35	852	5.8
23	26	49	15	67-1	9	3	120	3.4
622	1071	11,693	433	883-8	154	59	2829	8.3
48	81	129	27	102-0	11	10	198	4.6
		45	46	63-1			98	2.3
		8	7	14-0			20	3.3
341	667	1308	221	414-6	53	68	1466	8.0
29	43	72	10	29-1	1	4	86	9.9
		21,620	4100	2592-24			14,522	15.1
		4104	770	546-8			2673	16.2
			74	182			910	19.4
			6	17			61	20.3
		120	150	196-8			493	8.2
22	29	51	17	25-0	7	3	132	5.5
		5798	1026	3044-94			8766	9.6
		763	127	508-26			1142	8.8
			142	15	94-0		171	4.4
84	176	260	96	225-3	33	11	477	5.1
1	8	9	5	21-0	1	0	29	3.2

INDIVIDUAL REGULAR-SEASON RECORDS

MOST POINTS

Season	2,338	John Havlicek	1970-71
Game	60	Larry Bird vs. Atlanta	
		(at New Orleans)	March 12, 1985
Half	37	Larry Bird vs. Atlanta	
		(at New Orleans)	March 12, 1985
Quarter	24	Larry Bird vs. Indiana	March 30, 1983
Overtime	12	Bob Cousy at Syracuse	February 2, 1951
Average	28.9	John Havlicek	1970-71

MOST REBOUNDS

Season	1,930	Bill Russell	1963-64
Game	51	Bill Russell vs. Syracuse	February 5, 1960
Half	32	Bill Russell vs. Philadelphia	November 16, 1957
Quarter	17	Bill Russell vs. Philadelphia	November 16, 1957
		Bill Russell vs. Cincinnati	December 12, 1958
		Bill Russell vs. Syracuse	February 5, 1960
Average	24.7	Bill Russell	1963-64

MOST ASSISTS

Season	715	Bob Cousy	1959-60
Game	28	Bob Cousy vs. Minneapolis	February 27, 1959
Half	19	Bob Cousy vs. Minneapolis	February 27, 1959
Quarter	12	Bob Cousy vs. Minneapolis	February 27, 1959
Average	9.5	Bob Cousy	1959-60

MOST PERSONAL FOULS

Season	356	Charlie Scott	1975-76
Quarter	5	Jim Loscutoff vs. Cincinnati	November 12, 1962

MOST MINUTES PLAYED

Season	3,698	John Havlicek	1971-72
Average	45.4	John Havlicek	1970-71

LONGEST CONSECUTIVE GAMES STREAK

	488	Jo Jo White	Jan. 21, 1972–
			Jan. 29, 1978

HIGHEST FIELD GOAL PERCENTAGE

Season	.609	Cedric Maxwell	1979-80 (457-750)

HIGHEST FREE THROW PERCENTAGE (minimum of 100 attempts)

Season	.932	Bill Sharman	1958-59 (342-367)

MOST CONSECUTIVE FREE THROWS MADE

	59	Larry Bird	Nov. 9, 1987–
			Dec. 4, 1987

MOST DISQUALIFICATIONS

	19	Tom Sanders	1964-65

MOST BLOCKS

Season	214	Robert Parish	1980-81
Game	9	Kevin McHale at New Jersey	April 16, 1982
		Robert Parish vs. Atlanta	March 17, 1982
		Kevin McHale at Chicago	January 21, 1983

MOST STEALS

Season	166	Larry Bird	1985-86
Game	9	Larry Bird at Utah	February 18, 1985

	YEARS		GAMES	MIN.	FIELD GOALS MADE	FIELD GOAL ATTEMPTS	PCT.	FREE THROWS MADE	FREE THROWS ATT.	PCT.
Fred Scolari 5'-10" San Francisco '43 b. 3/1/22	1	54-55	59	619	76	249	.305	39	49	.796
Playoffs	1	55	5	29	4	15	.267	4	5	.800
Charlie Scott 6'-6" North Carolina '70 b. 12/15/48	3	75-78	156	5574	1124	2528	.445	480	626	.767
Playoffs	2	76-77	27	970	163	412	.396	99	124	.798
Ed Searcy 6'-6" St. John's '74 b. 4/17/52	1	75-76	4	12	2	6	.333	2	2	1.000
Jim Seminoff 6'-2" Southern California b. 1920	2	48-50	123		238	770	.309	293	407	.720
Earl Shannon 5'-11" Rhode Island b. 11/23/26 (Played 5 games for Boston, 27 for Providence in 1948-49.)	1	48-49	32		34	127	.268	39	58	.672
Howard Shannon 6'-3" Kansas '48 b. 6/10/23	1	49-50	67		222	646	.344	143	182	.786
Bill Sharman 6'-1" Southern California '50 b. 5/25/26	10	51-61	680	21,793	4620	10,807	.428	3047	3451	.883
Playoffs	10	52-61	78	2573	538	1262	.426	370	406	.911
Brian Shaw 6'-6" Cal–Santa Barbara '88 b. 3/22/66	1	88-89	82	2301	297	686	.433	109	132	.826
Playoffs	1	89	3	124	22	43	.512	7	9	.778
Jerry Sichting 6'-1" Purdue '79 b. 11/29/56	3	85-88	184	3532	481	892	.539	106	120	.883
Playoffs (Also played in 26 regular-season games for Portland, 1987-88.)	2	86-87	41	612	62	143	.434	11	17	.647
Larry Siegfried 6'-3" Ohio State '61 b. 5/22/39	7	63-70	466	11,401	1960	4747	.413	1500	1755	.855
Playoffs	6	64-69	79	1826	301	753	.400	256	307	.834
Paul Silas 6'-7" Creighton '64 b. 7/12/43	4	72-76	325	10,540	1367	3112	.439	1010	1394	.725
Playoffs	4	73-76	60	2232	208	492	.423	147	197	.746
Connie Simmons 6'-8" b. 3/15/25 (Played 32 games for Boston, 13 for Baltimore in 1947-48.)	2	46-48	105		408	1313	.311	190	297	.640
John Simmons 6'-1" New York University b. 1922	1	46-47	60		120	429	.280	78	127	.614
Garfield Smith 6'-9" Kentucky '68 b. 11/18/45	2	70-72	63	415	70	182	.390	28	87	.322
Playoffs	1	72	4	6	1	5	.200	0	3	.000
Art Spector 6'-4" Villanova b. 10/17/20	4	46-50	169		322	1149	.280	208	362	.575
Playoffs	1	48	3		2	9	.222	2	4	.500
Kevin Stacom 6'-4" Providence '74 b. 9/4/51	5	74-79	296	3878	679	1601	.424	210	272	.772
Playoffs	3	75-77	26	227	16	53	.302	9	12	.750
Ed Stanczak (Moose) 6'-1" b. 8/15/21	1	50-51	17		11	48	.229	35	43	.814
Gene Stump 6'-2" DePaul '47 b. 11/13/23	2	47-49	99		252	827	.305	116	167	.695
Playoffs	1	48	3		1	3	.333	0	0	.000
Ben Swain 6'-8" Texas Southern '58 b. 11/13/33	1	58-59	58	708	99	244	.406	67	110	.609
Playoffs	1	59	5	27	2	6	.333	1	2	.500
Dan Swartz 6'-4" Morehead State '56 b. 12/23/34	1	62-63	39	335	57	150	.380	61	72	.847
Playoffs	1	63	1	4	0	0	.000	0	0	.000
Earl Tatum 6'-6" Marquette '76 b. 7/26/53	1	78-79	3	38	8	20	.400	4	5	.800
Tom Thacker 6'-3" Cincinnati '63 b. 11/2/41	1	67-68	65	782	114	272	.419	43	84	.512
Playoffs	1	68	17	81	7	24	.292	2	7	.286
David Thirdkill 6'-8" Bradley '82 b. 4/12/60	2	85-87	62	463	64	129	.496	60	100	.600
Playoffs	1	86	13	47	6	18	.333	5	11	.455
John Thompson 6'-10" Providence '64 b. 9/2/41	2	64-66	74	771	98	239	.410	66	111	.595
Playoffs	2	65-66	6	32	3	14	.214	7	7	1.000
Darren Tillis 6'-11" Cleveland State '82 b. 2/23/60	1	82-83	15	44	7	23	.304	2	6	.333
Lou Tsioropoulos 6'-5" Kentucky '53 b. 8/31/30	3	56-59	157	2977	337	1070	.315	236	329	.717
Playoffs	1	58	11	239	25	85	.294	19	29	.655
Andre Turner 5'-11" Memphis State '86 b. 12/13/64	1	86-87	3	18	2	5	.400	0	0	.000
Kelvin Upshaw 6'-2" Utah '86 b. 1/24/63	1	88-89	23	473	73	149	.490	14	20	.700
Playoffs	1	89	3	24	5	12	.417	0	0	.000
Virgil Vaughn 6'-4" Kentucky Wesleyan	1	46-47	17		15	78	.192	15	28	.536

OFF.	DEF.	TOT.	ASSISTS	PERS. FOULS/ DISQ.	STEALS	BLOCKED SHOTS	PTS.	AVG.
			77	93	76-0			191	3.2
			5	3	7-0			12	2.4
182	468	650	680	608-22	214	42	2728	17.5
38	76	114	109	138-14	34	10	425	15.7
0	0	0	1	4-0	0	0	6	1.5
			478	349			769	6.3
			44	33			107	3.3
			174	148			587	8.8
		2683	2062	1839-24			12,287	18.1
		285	201	220-6			1446	18.5
119	257	376	472	211-1	78	27	703	8.6
2	15	17	18	11-0	3	0	51	17.0
54	162	216	435	272-0	104	1	1083	5.9
10	26	36	73	54-0	14	0	136	3.3
		1318	1532	1108-7			5420	11.6
		199	209	249-5			858	10.9
		4004	864	899-10			3744	11.5
		763	168	202-4			563	9.4
			86	252			1006	9.6
			29	78			318	5.3
		132	17	75-0			168	2.7
		1	0	1-0			2	0.5
			143	351			852	5.0
			0	9			6	2.0
168	275	443	440	325-0	96	14	1568	5.3
9	10	19	21	24-0	5	0	41	1.6
		34	6	6-0			57	3.4
			74	168			620	6.3
			0	2			2	0.7
		262	29	127-3			265	4.6
			14	1	4-0			5	1.0
			88	21	92-0			175	4.5
			0	0	0-0			0	0.0
1	3	4	1	7-0	0	1	20	6.7
		161	69	165-2			271	4.2
		17	8	23-0			16	0.9
29	55	84	17	66-0	12	3	188	3.0
1	7	8	3	5-0	2	0	17	1.3
		260	19	156-1			262	3.5
		16	1	4-0			13	2.2
4	5	9	2	8-0	0	2	16	1.1
		751	165	451-14			910	5.8
		64	14	40-4			69	6.3
1	1	2	1	1-0	0	0	4	1.3
6	30	36	97	62-1	19	3	162	7.0
0	2	2	5	4-0	1	0	10	3.3
			10	18			45	2.6

CELTICS' GREATEST INDIVIDUAL REGULAR-SEASON PERFORMANCES

SCORING

60	Larry Bird vs. Atlanta (at New Orleans)	March 12, 1985
56	Kevin McHale vs. Detroit	March 3, 1985
53	Larry Bird vs. Indiana	March 30, 1983
51	Sam Jones at Detroit	October 29, 1965
50	Larry Bird at Dallas	March 10, 1986
49	Larry Bird vs. Washington	January 27, 1988
49	Larry Bird at Phoenix	February 15, 1988
48	Larry Bird vs. Houston	March 17, 1985
48	Larry Bird vs. Portland	January 27, 1985
48	Larry Bird vs. Atlanta	December 9, 1984
47	Larry Bird vs. New York	April 12, 1987
47	Larry Bird vs. Portland	February 14, 1986
47	Larry Bird vs. Detroit	November 27, 1985
47	Larry Bird vs. Milwaukee	April 12, 1985

FIELD GOALS MADE

22	Larry Bird vs. New York	April 12, 1987
22	Larry Bird vs. Atlanta (at New Orleans)	March 12, 1985
22	Kevin McHale vs. Detroit	March 3, 1985
21	Larry Bird at Portland	February 14, 1986
21	Larry Bird vs. Indiana	March 30, 1983
21	Sam Jones at Detroit	October 29, 1965
20	Larry Bird vs. Atlanta	December 9, 1984
20	Larry Bird vs. Washington	January 27, 1988

FREE THROWS MADE

20	Nate Archibald vs. Chicago	January 16, 1980
19	Cedric Maxwell vs. New Jersey	January 14, 1979
19	John Havlicek vs. Seattle	February 6, 1970
19	Frank Ramsey at Detroit	December 3, 1957
19	Bill Sharman at Philadelphia	March 8, 1956

ASSISTS

28	Bob Cousy vs. Minneapolis	February 27, 1959
23	Nate Archibald vs. Denver	February 5, 1982
21	Bob Cousy vs. St. Louis	December 21, 1960
19	Nate Archibald at San Antonio	October 23, 1979
19	Bob Cousy vs. Cincinnati	February 19, 1963
19	Bob Cousy vs. Syracuse	November 24, 1956
18	Nate Archibald at Seattle	December 16, 1982
18	Bob Cousy at New York	November 21, 1959
18	Bob Cousy vs. New York	January 18, 1953

REBOUNDS

51	Bill Russell vs. Syracuse	February 5, 1960
49	Bill Russell vs. Philadelphia	November 16, 1957
49	Bill Russell vs. Detroit	March 11, 1965
43	Bill Russell vs. Los Angeles	January 20, 1963
41	Bill Russell vs. Syracuse	February 12, 1958
41	Bill Russell vs. San Francisco	March 14, 1965
40	Bill Russell vs. Cincinnati	December 12, 1958
40	Bill Russell vs. Philadelphia	February 12, 1961

	YEARS	GAMES	MIN.	FIELD GOALS MADE	FIELD GOAL ATTEMPTS	PCT.	FREE THROWS MADE	FREE THROWS ATT.	PCT.
Sam Vincent 6'-2" Michigan State '85 b. 5/18/63	2	85-87	103	806	119	298	.399	116	125	.928
Playoffs	2	86-87	26	182	31	84	.369	33	41	.805
Brady Walker 6'-6" Brigham Young '48 b. 3/15/21	2	49-50	134		382	999	.382	144	217	.664
Mike Wallace (Red) 6'-1" Scranton b. 7/12/18 (Played 24 games for Boston, 37 for Toronto in 1946-47.)	1	46-47	61		225	809	.278	106	196	.541
Bill Walton 6'-11" U.C.L.A. '74 b. 11/5/52	2	85-87	90	1658	241	437	.551	152	217	.700
Playoffs	2	86-87	28	393	66	118	.559	24	37	.649
Gerry Ward 6'-4" Boston College '63 b. 9/6/41	1	64-65	3	30	2	18	.111	1	1	1.000
Kermit Washington 6'-8" American '73 b. 9/17/51	1	77-78	32	866	137	263	.521	102	136	.750
Ron Watts 6'-6" Wake Forest '65 b. 5/21/43	2	65-67	28	92	12	46	.261	16	23	.696
Playoffs	1	67	1	5	1	6	.167	1	2	.500
Scott Wedman 6'-7" Colorado '74 b. 7/29/52	5	82-87	271	4026	757	1630	.464	137	190	.721
Playoffs	4	83-86	56	784	147	305	.482	35	54	.648
Rick Weitzman 6'-2" Northeastern '67 b. 4/30/46	1	67-68	25	75	12	46	.261	9	13	.692
Playoffs	1	68	3	5	2	3	.667	0	0	.000
Paul Westphal 6'-4" Southern California '72 b. 11/30/50	3	72-75	224	3228	669	1357	.493	298	395	.754
Playoffs	3	73-75	40	533	103	220	.486	28	40	.700
Jo Jo White 6'-3" Kansas '69 b. 11/16/46	10	69-79	717	26,770	5648	12,782	.442	1892	2270	.833
Playoffs	6	72-77	80	3428	732	1629	.449	256	309	.828
Lucian Whittaker (Skippy) 6'-1" Kentucky '52	1	54-55	3	15	1	6	.167	0	0	.000
Sidney Wicks 6'-9" U.C.L.A. '71 b. 9/19/49	2	76-78	163	5055	897	1939	.463	527	793	.665
Playoffs	1	77	9	261	41	81	.519	34	47	.723
Art Williams (Hambone) 6'-1" California Poly '63 b. 9/29/39	4	70-74	303	4057	494	1098	.450	220	290	.759
Playoffs	3	72-74	33	425	56	138	.406	28	36	.778
Earl Williams 6'-7" Winston-Salem '74 b. 3/24/51	1	78-79	20	273	54	123	.439	14	24	.583
Ray Williams 6'-3" Minnesota '77 b. 10/14/54	1	84-85	23	459	55	143	.385	31	46	.674
Sly Williams 6'-7" Rhode Island '80 b. 1/26/58	1	85-86	6	54	5	21	.238	7	12	.583
Willie Williams 6'-7" Florida State '70 b. 7/28/46 (Played 9 games for Cincinnati, 1970-71, 7 for Boston.)	1	70-71	16	56	6	32	.188	3	5	.600
Bobby Wilson 6'-1" Wichita State '74 b. 1/15/51	1	76-77	25	131	19	59	.322	11	13	.846

OPPONENTS' GREATEST INDIVIDUAL REGULAR-SEASON PERFORMANCES

SCORING

64 Elgin Baylor at Minneapolis...................... November 8, 1959
62 Wilt Chamberlain, Philadelphia at Boston .... January 14, 1962
55 Kareem Abdul-Jabbar at Milwaukee..............December 10, 1971
54 Dominique Wilkins at Atlanta .... February 3, 1987

FIELD GOALS MADE

27 Wilt Chamberlain, Philadelphia at Boston .... January 14, 1962
25 Elgin Baylor at Minneapolis...................... November 8, 1959
25 Wilt Chamberlain, Phil. vs. Boston at NY .... February 23, 1960

FREE THROWS MADE

22 Richie Guerin, New York at Boston .... February 11, 1961
20 Kareem Abdul-Jabbar, Milwaukee at Boston .... March 8, 1970

ASSISTS

25 Kevin Porter at Detroit .... March 9, 1979
21 Clem Haskins, Chicago at Boston (OT) .... December 6, 1969

REBOUNDS

55 Wilt Chamberlain at Philadelphia................. November 24, 1960
43 Wilt Chamberlain at Philadelphia................... March 6, 1965
42 Wilt Chamberlain at Philadelphia .... January 15, 1960
42 Wilt Chamberlain at Philadelphia .... January 14, 1966
42 Wilt Chamberlain at Los Angeles .... March 7, 1969

OFF.	DEF.	TOT.	ASSISTS	PERS. FOULS/ DISQ.	STEALS	BLOCKED SHOTS	PTS.	AVG.
16	59	75	128	92-0	30	5	355	3.4
4	15	19	24	22-0	5	2	96	3.7
		354	220	183-2			908	6.8
			58	167-0			556	9.1
147	428	575	174	223-1	39	116	634	7.0
34	100	134	37	68-1	9	16	156	5.6
		5	6	6-0			5	1.7
105	230	335	42	114-2	28	40	376	11.8
		39	2	17-0			40	1.4
		2	0	3-0			3	3.0
196	377	573	281	434-1	110	47	1689	6.2
60	82	142	58	94-1	29	3	345	6.2
		10	8	8-0			33	1.3
		1	1	0-0			4	1.3
		373	475	453-1			1636	7.3
		41	72	82-2			234	5.9
		3071	3686	1776-21			13,188	18.3
		348	452	241-3			1720	21.5
		1	1	4-0			2	0.7
491	1006	1497	340	649-23	131	107	2321	14.2
26	57	83	16	37-2	13	3	118	13.1
		758	959	622-4			1208	4.0
		78	103	75-1			140	4.2
41	64	105	12	41-0	12	9	122	6.1
16	41	57	90	56-1	30	5	147	6.4
7	8	15	2	15-0	1	1	17	2.8
		10	2	8-0			15	0.9
3	6	9	14	19-0	3	0	49	2.0

CELTICS' OWNERSHIP

1946–1948	Walter Brown/Boston Garden-Arena Corporation
1948–1950	Walter Brown
1950–1964	Walter Brown/Lou Pieri
1964–1965	Lou Pieri/Marjorie Brown
1965–1968	Marvin Kratter/National Equities
1968–1969	Ballantine Brewery
1969–1971	E. E. (Woody) Erdman/Trans-National Communications
1971–1972	Investors' Funding Corporation
1972–1974	Bob Schmertz/Leisure Technology
1974–1975	Bob Schmertz/Irv Levin
1975–1978	Irv Levin
1978–1979	John Y. Brown/Harry Mangurian, Jr.
1979–1983	Harry Mangurian, Jr.
1983–present	Don Gaston, Paul Dupee, Jr., Alan Cohen

YEAR-BY-YEAR ATTENDANCE AT BOSTON GARDEN

Year	Games	Attendance	Average
1946-47	30*	108,240	3,608
1947-48	24*	90,264	3,761
1948-49	29*	144,275	4,975
1949-50	26*	110,552	4,252
1950-51	32*	197,888	6,184
1951-52	29*	160,167	5,523
1952-53	24	161,808	6,742
1953-54	21	156,912	7,472
1954-55	25	175,675	7,027
1955-56	26	209,645	8,064
1956-57	25	262,918	10,517
1957-58	29	240,943	8,308
1958-59	30	244,642	8,165
1959-60	27	209,374	7,755
1960-61	28	201,569	7,199
1961-62	28	191,855	6,852
1962-63	30	262,581	8,753
1963-64	30	223,347	7,445
1964-65	30	246,529	8,318
1965-66	31	246,189	7,941
1966-67	31	322,690	10,409
1967-68	37	320,788	8,670
1968-69	36	322,130	8,948
1969-70	37	277,632	7,504
1970-71	39	313,768	8,045
1971-72	41	346,701	8,456
1972-73	39	423,234	10,852
1973-74	32	355,261	11,102
1974-75	34	452,421	13,307
1975-76	36	484,039	13,446
1976-77	35	453,672	12,962
1977-78	36	437,937	12,165
1978-79	41	407,926	10,193
1979-80	39	565,105	14,490
1980-81	36	536,883	14,913
1981-82	38	582,160	15,320
1982-83	38	582,160	15,320
1983-84	38	565,820	14,890
1984-85	38	565,820	14,890
1985-86	38	565,820	14,890
1986-87	38	565,820	14,890
1987-88	38	565,820	14,890
1988-89	38	565,820	14,890

* Includes games at Boston Arena.

CELTICS IN THE ALL-STAR GAME

APPEARANCES

PLAYER	TOTAL	CONSECUTIVE	FIRST	LAST
Bob Cousy	13	13	1951	1963
John Havlicek	13	13	1966	1978
Bill Russell	12	12	1958	1969
Larry Bird	9	9	1980	1988
Bill Sharman	8	8	1953	1960
Robert Parish	7	7	1981	1987
Jo Jo White	7	7	1971	1977
Dave Cowens	6	5	1972	1978
Tom Heinsohn	6	5	1957	1965
Ed Macauley	6	6	1951	1956
Sam Jones	5	3	1962	1968
Kevin McHale	5	4	1984	1989
Nate Archibald	3	3	1980	1982
Danny Ainge	1	—	1988	1988
Dennis Johnson	1	—	1985	1985
Don Barksdale	1	—	1953	1953
Bailey Howell	1	—	1967	1967
Paul Silas	1	—	1975	1975

COACHING

Red Auerbach	11	(7 wins, 4 losses)	1957	1967
K.C. Jones	4	(2 wins, 2 losses)	1984	1987
Tom Heinsohn	4	(2 wins, 2 losses)	1972	1976
Bill Fitch	1	(1 win, 0 losses)	1982	1982

MOST VALUABLE PLAYERS

1951	Ed Macauley
1954	Bob Cousy
1955	Bill Sharman
1957	Bob Cousy
1963	Bill Russell
1973	Dave Cowens
1981	Nate Archibald
1982	Larry Bird

The All-Star Game has been held in Boston four times: 1951, 1952, 1957 and 1964.

CELTICS IN NAISMITH MEMORIAL BASKETBALL HALL OF FAME
Springfield, Massachusetts

In order of election:

Ed Macauley (1960)	Bill Sharman (1975)
Andy Phillip (1961)	Frank Ramsey (1981)
John (Honey) Russell (1964)	John Havlicek (1983)
Walter Brown (1965)	Sam Jones (1983)
Bill Mokray (1965)	Tom Heinsohn (1985)
Alvin (Doggie) Julian (1967)	Bob Houbregs (1986)
Arnold (Red) Auerbach (1968)	Peter Maravich (1986)
Bob Cousy (1970)	Clyde Lovelette (1987)
Bill Russell (1974)	

NBA TITLES BY FRANCHISE

Team	Number	Last	Coach
Boston Celtics	16	1985-86	K.C. Jones
Minneapolis—Los Angles Lakers	11		Pat Riley
Philadelphia—Golden State Warriors	3	1974-75	Al Attles
Syracuse Nets—Philadelphia 76ers	3	1982-83	Billy Cunningham
New York Knickerbockers	2		
Baltimore Bullets*	1	1947-48	Buddy Jeannette
Milwaukee Bucks	1	1970-71	Larry Costello
Portland Trail Blazers	1	1976-77	Jack Ramsay
Rochester Royals—Sacramento Kings	1	1950-51	Lester Harrison
St. Louis—Atlanta Hawks	1	1957-58	Alex Hannum
Seattle Supersonics	1	1978-79	Lenny Wilkens
Washington Bullets	1	1977-78	Dick Motta

*Franchise disbanded on Nov. 27, 1954

CELTICS' ASSISTANT COACHES

1946-47–1947-48	Danny Silva
1948-49–1949-50	Henry McCarthy
1949-50	Art Spector
1972-73–1976-77	John Killilea
1977-78	Tom (Satch) Sanders
1978-79	Bob MacKinnon
1977-78–1982-83	K.C. Jones
1980-81–1987-88	Jimmy Rodgers
1983-84–present	Chris Ford
1984-85–1987-88	Ed Badger
1988-89–present	Lanny Van Eman